T0380677

FINDING EXCELLENCE

A Practical Guide to Fostering Goodwill Dissent
&
Human Flourishing at Work

GORDEN SIMANGO, (DTL)

WESTBOW
PRESS®
A DIVISION OF THOMAS NELSON
& ZONDERVAN

WestBow Press books may be ordered through booksellers or by contacting:

WestBow Press
A Division of Thomas Nelson & Zondervan
1663 Liberty Drive
Bloomington, IN 47403
www.westbowpress.com
844-714-3454

Interior Image Credit: Clarrisa de Wet

Scripture quotations are taken from the Amplified® Bible, Copyright © 1954, 1958, 1962, 1964, 1965, 1987 by The Lockman Foundation. Used by permission.

ISBN: 979-8-3850-1935-9 (sc)
ISBN: 979-8-3850-1936-6 (e)

Library of Congress Control Number: 2024903472

Print information available on the last page.

WestBow Press rev. date: 02/28/2024

Contents

Finally, believers, whatever is true, whatever is honorable *and* worthy of respect, whatever is right *and* confirmed by God's word, whatever is pure *and* wholesome, whatever is lovely *and* brings peace, whatever is admirable *and* of good repute; if there is **any excellence,** if there is anything worthy of praise, think *continually* on these things [center your mind on them, and implant them in your heart]. The things which you have learned and received and heard and seen in me, practice these things [in daily life], and the God [who is the source] of peace *and* well-being will be with you.

Philippians 4:8-9

Acknowledgments

God deserves the glory for enabling me to complete this book. This book is based on my dissertation for the Doctor of Transformational Leadership (DTL) program at Bakke Graduate University (BGU), Dallas, Texas, USA. I will be eternally grateful to Tendai (my wife), Ropafadzo (my daughter), and Immanuel (my son) for their unending love and encouragement.

I would like to give special thanks to the book's editor, Dr. Zachary Hamilton. Dr. Zachary, together with Dr. Belete Mebratu, served as my dissertation co-supervisors at BGU during my DTL program. I am grateful to both. I am also indebted to Dr. Martine Audéoud, my academic advisor in the DTL program, for her invaluable counsel and support. Most of the interviews in this book were conducted with individuals affiliated with the Society for Human Resource Management in Ethiopia (SHRME), the Ethiopian Berhane Wongel Baptist Church (EBWBC), and the Ethiopian Mulu Wongel Amagnoch Church Development Commission (EMWACDC). Multiple interviews were also held with students at Bakke Graduate University, and influential people from Africa, the Middle East, and Latin America who have made significant contributions to their respective regions. Pastor Dr. Fekadu Fetene, a BGU alumnus and former General Secretary of the EBWBC, and Dr. Kebede Gonfa, the organization's current General Secretary (at the time of writing this book), both deserve my appreciation. I would like to thank Dr. Yohannes Hailemariam, a former commissioner at EMWACDC and a fellow DTL student at BGU (then). I would also like to extend my gratitude to acting Commissioner Emiru Mulatu, who took over from Commissioner Yohannes right as I was getting started on my research. I would like to express my appreciation to Ato Girum Ketema, former co-chair of the board of the Ethiopian Society for Human Resource Management (SHRME). I appreciate your assistance in sending my online survey to the SHRME constituency and arranging the validation workshop for my research results that SHRME hosted at the Mado Hotel in Addis Ababa on the evening of Wednesday, December 14, 2022. Clarissa de Wet, you did a wonderful job of simplifying the principles presented in this book through your skills in illustrations and cartoons.

I am grateful to my research assistant, Ato Biraanu Gammachu, a former postgraduate student at the Institute for Peace and Security Studies (IPSS) at Addis Ababa University in Ethiopia.

This book is informed by my 26 years of experience working in the nonprofit sector. During that time, I witnessed employees struggling to convey their contributions and sentiments up the organizational hierarchy. This was due to employers routinely stifling dissenting voices knowingly or unconsciously. I saw people having difficulties conveying their contributions and feelings out of fear. People have an intrinsic urge to be seen and acknowledged. Employees can give the best of their ideas and apply their brains to an organization's mission and vision when the environment in which they work encourages benevolent dissent and provides a safe space for it. An environment that fosters goodwill dissent helps employees to contribute the best of their ideas and apply their minds to the mission and vision of the organization.

Only pseudonyms are used in this book

This book is a valuable resource for anyone who wants to improve their work life or the work lives of others. It provides practical advice on how to maximize goodwill dissent and appreciating the strengths of others, to edify organizations and human relations.

The book is written for anyone who wants to improve their leadership skills. It provides practical advice and real-life examples that can be applied to any leadership position. Whether you are a student, a seasoned professional, a parent, or a CEO, this book will help you to become a more effective leader.

The book's focus is wide. It covers:

- The need for fostering feedback and how to,
- The need for fostering goodwill dissent and how to,
- Human flourishing,
- Emotional wellbeing,
- Finding excellence and investing in it,
- Practicing and sustaining excellence,
- Leadership perspectives on Constructive workplace dissent, Emotional wellbeing, and Human flourishing.

The book is clear and concise in style, and it is easy to follow. The author provides helpful tips and advice, draws from the experiences of others, and shares his own experiences as a leader. Some concepts are communicated through a cartoon and illustrations.

Maybe you are a worker who has been holding back your suggestions for fear of retaliation or pushback because you have experienced it before, or you have seen others experiencing it. Do you ever get the impression that the things you were trained to do may have been effective in the past, but are now redundant or that your organization could benefit from an idea you have, and you are holding back on – and perhaps now you do not care anymore? Do you always think of ways to improve your work, but you never have the nerve to bring them up? You may benefit your organization, yourself and others', by applying the ideas and insights presented in this book.

Do you approach your job as something enjoyable or as a contractual obligation? If the second scenario describes you, you may be happy to hear that it is possible to enjoy your work while simultaneously performing at a level that is higher than you. Finding a higher purpose and meaning in your profession and happiness for yourself and others may alter your life. I am not implying that we do not all need to earn money to make a living and to provide for ourselves and our families; I am just saying that it is possible to have both. Some employees work because they must. They would probably quit their jobs if they won the lottery tomorrow. Some generally accept that work is a burden, a requirement, something we undertake on a contractual basis in exchange for a benefit that enables us to support our families and live comfortably. Some workers stop working as soon as their contractually required hours permit. This relationship between the employee and the employer is purely transactional. In this book, I demonstrate how you can not only provide for your loved ones but also add a new dimension to your life by discovering the genuine joy that can be found in your work, and a higher purpose.

Perhaps you are already in a managerial position and though competent, you fail to fully leverage the knowledge and experience of your subordinates. You also know that the organizational culture has never valued employees speaking up, and you have no idea how to course correct it. I hope that the professional experiences and techniques shared in this book will inspire you to help your staff to speak up and provide the finest of their ideas.

BIBLICAL FOUNDATIONS FOR THE BOOK

It honors God, who created human beings and gave them work to do both individually and together, when employers actively invite others to speak the truth in love, and to criticize constructively. The Bible reveals that Jesus Christ "came from the Father, full of grace and truth," demonstrating "gentleness and respect" (Ephesians 4:15; John 1:14; 1 Peter 3:15).

There are many passages in the Bible that relate to goodwill dissent and human flourishing. Reflections in this prologue are limited to the Lord's prayer found in Matthew 6:9-13. This prayer has the same power now as it did when it was first said. The prayer hints about how people must speak to authority – honoring the name of the Father "Hallowed be your name" (Matthew 6:9). This reveals the importance of expressing truth with respect to authority. The prayer also teaches people to do unto others as they would have them do unto them - a very difficult yard stick to measure up to, but a necessity for our own healing and forging forward. In this the Lord's prayer, the measure of people's forgiveness, is intimately linked to the capacity and willingness to forgive others (Matthew 6:12). The petitioner recognizes the importance of seeking mercy, but also the need to adopt the same standard that people expect of others, seeking to be heard, and humbling ourselves to hear others who are seeking to be heard too – forgive our trespasses, as we forgive those who trespass against us.

Christ says, "These things I have spoken to you, that my joy may be in you, and that your joy may be full" (John 15:11). It pleases the Lord God when things go well for His people; even when His people circumstances are difficult, that their joy is not lost. In a workplace, leaders and employees must remain receptive to what God is calling them to, to see the image of God in the other. God only is the source of a receptive heart. "And I will give them one heart [a new heart] and put a new spirit within them. I will take from them the heart of stone, and will give them a heart of flesh [that is responsive to My touch]" (Ezekiel 11:19, 26). "I will put My law within them, and I will write it on their hearts; and I will be their God, and they will be My people. (Jeremiah 31:33). For this is the covenant we have with God (Hebrews 8:10).

Key Glossary Terms

APPRECIATIVE INQUIRY (AI)

According to Cooperrider and Whitney (2005), *AI* is the cooperative, coevolutionary search for the best in people, their organizations, and the world around them. It involves systematic discovery of what gives life to an organization or a community when it is most effective and most capable in economic, ecological, and human terms. (p. 8)

CONSTRUCTIVE CRITICISM

According to Martins (2022), *constructive criticism* "focuses on providing constructive feedback, supported by specific examples, to help you improve in some area. Constructive criticism should be offered in a friendly manner with good intentions" (para. 3).

Constructive Workplace Dissent: According to Campeau (2016), *constructive workplace dissent* refers to "the ability to disagree [or act] in a positive way while maintaining connection, trust, and respect for others' points of view" (Campeau, para. 4).
　　See also Goodwill Dissent

Emotional Wellbeing: (*See Psychological Safety).* In the case of this book, the term Emotional Wellbeing is used interchangeably with the term Psychological safety.

Finding Excellence: Finding the talents, special skills, and knowledge employees are contributing to the organization (abundance), and maximizing on these as opposed to their shortfalls (deficits) only.

Goodwill Dissent: Speaking up for or against the status quo with the best intentions. In the case of this book, Goodwill dissent is at times used interchangeably with the term Constructive Workplace Dissent

Human Flourishing: Achieving one's full potential whilst putting one's best self forward in service of others and participating in the kinds of relationships and pursuits that one holds dearest and most meaningful. Individual effort and an encouraging setting are prerequisites for succeeding.

Joy at Work (JAW): This is related to Bakke's Joy at work model which is a model premised on his "passion... to make work exciting, rewarding, stimulating and enjoyable" (p. 13). Bakke (2005). Employees who have a gratifying sense of mission and purpose and who seek a higher-end purpose than monetary reward alone have found JAW. JAW also means employee talents flourish at work.

Psychological Safety: According to the Centre for Creative Leadership (n.d.), psychological safety is a common conviction held by members of a team that others on the team would not disgrace, reject, or punish you for speaking up... [this] doesn't imply that everyone is always polite. It means you embrace controversy and speak up, confident in the knowledge that your team has your back and you have theirs. When people are afraid to talk about efforts that aren't working, the organization isn't prepared to avoid failure. (Centre for Creative Leadership, n.d.)

PSYCHOLOGICAL SAFETY

According to Thomas (2022), *psychological safety* is defined as, "being able to show and employ one's self without fear of negative consequences of self-image, status, or career. In other words, psychological safety means team members feel accepted and respected within their current roles" (para. 2).

TALENT(S)

The definition of *talent* according to the Merriam-Webster (n.d.) dictionary is

> 1a: a special often athletic, creative, or artistic aptitude
>   b: general intelligence or mental power: Ability
> 2: the natural endowments of a person
> 3: a person of talent or a group of persons of talent in a field or activity.

Abstract

The cartoon in this section forms an abstract of this book. It introduces the leadership and management concepts I cover herein. The cartoon is informed by real-life situations in workplaces; and proffers a solution through
finding
EXCELLENCE,
and
GOODWILL DISSENT
to foster
HUMAN FLOURISHING

FIND EXCELLENCE

At this job, management met once a week with the employees to ask for their input and they listened and took into account what was spoken by them.

I believe that if we change this policy, we will be able to work together better as employees and be more productive to this company.

I had a place where I could express what I believe is right without being shot down. This formed a platform to complete my fellow employees and not compete with them.

Nandi, have you typed out and printed that report?

Yes sir, here it is.

Because the management was open with me I knew exactly what the duties I was expected to do and I did my very best to fulfil my duties.

I dont agree with how the factory is run. It is not fair on the workers there. To employ a factory manager with integrity will be a large step into having a more productive workforce in the factory.

They taught us that providing solutions, suggestions and options in dissent makes it constructive.

They would never impose something on their employees, but discuss and implement it causing the employees and employer to be of the same understanding.

Psychological safety is very important to them. Speaking truth is valuable and they are available emotionally to support their employees.

I am so grateful to be part of this company.

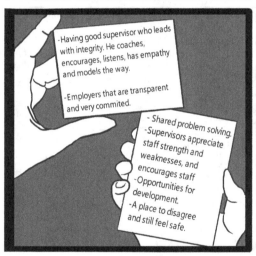

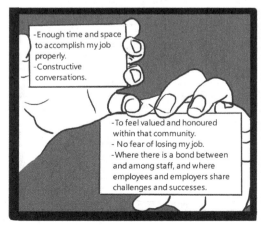

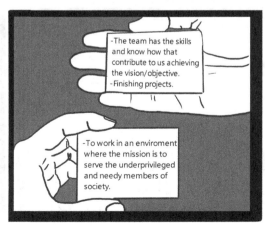

3. Invest and Resource

How will this look practically?

-Staff welfare programs.
-Work enviroment ie computers lights, chairs etc in condition for optimal work.
-Personal fellowship times.
-Give people picture of the end goal of desired outcome.

Organizational structures that lacks support for conductive working enviroments might not flourish human potential, psyc ological safety, joy at work and constructive workplace dissent.

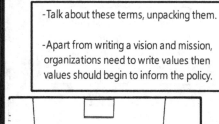

-Talk about these terms, unpacking them.

-Apart from writing a vision and mission, organizations need to write values then values should begin to inform the policy.

Workplaces must be places where one can learn something diffrent from what they know.

...And that is what Ergonomics is, and how it can influence your psychological health in your working enviroment.

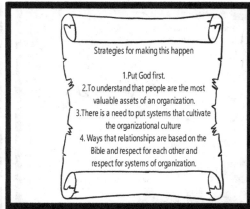

To promote joy at work, Psychological health and constructive workplace dissent, create a system in which positive behaviour in this is rewarded. Milestones in these areas are set and employees are rewarded when they reach them.

Strategies for making this happen

1. Put God first.
2. To understand that people are the most valuable assets of an organization.
3. There is a need to put systems that cultivate the organizational culture
4. Ways that relationships are based on the Bible and respect for each other and respect for systems of organization.

4.Practice and Sustain

What seeds need to be sown for an organization to embody the values of Joy at work, constructive workplace disscent and psychological safety.

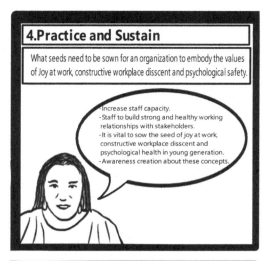

- Increase staff capacity.
- Staff to build strong and healthy working relationships with stakeholders.
- It is vital to sow the seed of joy at work, constructive workplace disscent and psychological health in young generation.
- Awareness creation about these concepts.

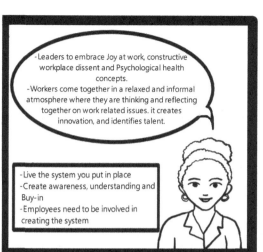

- Leaders to embrace Joy at work, constructive workplace dissent and Psychological health concepts.
- Workers come together in a relaxed and informal atmosphere where they are thinking and reflecting together on work related issues. it creates innovation, and identifies talent.

- Live the system you put in place
- Create awareness, understanding and Buy-in
- Employees need to be involved in creating the system

What needs to be done to ensure what is suggested survives?

- Sacrifice and commitment.
- Be patient with investments.
- Hear what God is saying at all stages
- Training.
- Staff well being.
- Repetition

- Recource the transformation/ renewal process- both financial and human resources.
- Invest in trust building
- Allow ideas from the periphery
- Ergonomics
- Pay staff well.
- Live staff care policy

What would your involvement be in ensuring that what you are proposing succeeds?

- Start with yourself in any change or transformation.
- Self involvement is critical.
- Be comitted to share ideas openly and in earnest.
- As a leader, one must pave the way for others to follow you.
- Work on your own accountability and responsibilities.
- Holding teams accountable.
- Speak up your Ideas.
- Assisting and helping others.
- Trust and respect others.
- Learn communication skills.
- Commiting to lifelong learning and adapting if need be.

What role will the organization play ensuring success?

- Maintain good connections and good relationships with others.
- Reporting failures and wrongdoings when needed.
- Supporting the system and teamwork.
- Influence others with good ideas.
- Be encouraging and supportive of others.
- Lead by example
- Be comfortable in standing up for what you believe in.
- Be accountable.
- Honest truthful critisisms.

EHIP framework for flourishing Employee talents based on Phillipians 4:8-9

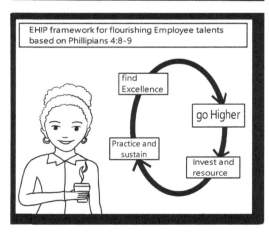

find Excellence

go Higher

Practice and sustain

Invest and resource

Chapter 1

FOSTERING FEEDBACK

In today's world, the autocratic leadership style *Do as I say not as I do* does not motivate employees and inspire results like it used to. During the current global reset, leaders are increasingly obligated to make room in a conversation for employees to constructively speak truth to them, and to allow employees to forge their own ideas. "But speaking the truth in love [in all things-both our speech and our lives expressing His truth], let us grow up in all *things* into Him [following His example] who is the Head—Christ" (Ephesians 4:15).

Both employers and employees can benefit much from receiving constructive feedback. Constructive feedback helps employees to continually develop their abilities and improve their performance. Likewise, constructive feedback helps employers to gain a better grasp of how employees are faring and to ensure that they render the appropriate support.

The need for constructive feedback from employees is true at the microscopic level as well as the organizational level; employees might be junior, but they are an important part of the organization system. Employees should be encouraged to give feedback to their managers and coworkers. This feedback can be helpful in identifying areas where the organization can improve. It can also help to build trust and communication between employees and managers.

Additionally, employers are obligated to find areas where employees are excelling (finding excellence) in their roles and responsibilities at work, and ride on these strengths (abundance) to encourage feedback (Philippians 4:8-9). Constructive feedback should be specific, timely, and actionable. It should focus on the employee's performance, not on their person; it should be offered in a respectful and helpful manner.

Goodwill dissent generates better work systems, better results and generates higher morale. Organizations are run by people; their views, perspectives, suggestions, knowledge, and talents help both the employers and employees to grow. Employers and employees must find amicable ways to encourage goodwill dissent. Employees in organizations sometimes feel like no one notices and listens, which may have a negative impact on morale and productivity.

Few studies have looked at how managers respond when workers criticize them or provide inventive solutions (Sijbom et al, 2015). This is notable since leaders have a crucial role in controlling and implementing employees' input that is deemed relevant for an organization, in addition to being crucial in inspiring employees to engage in innovation (Sijbom et al, 2015). Though well-intentioned, supervisors may first resist and push back on subordinates' suggestions because they may threaten established procedures. The way in which employees speak up to managers can elicit a variety of responses, depending on whether the employees speak up in a hostile or supportive manner. Employees would probably do well considering the complications of utilizing their voices responsibly rather than as an afterthought. Solomon the son of David, the King of Israel said, "Death and life are in the power of the tongue, and those who love it will eat its fruits" (Proverbs 18:12).

THE CRUX OF THE MATTER

Even while many workers want to feel that their work is meaningful and appreciated at their work, and they want to work in an environment that appreciates their abilities and talents; there is sometimes a disconnect between how organizations address this demand and how well they do so. There is less doubt that the need for workplaces to promote goodwill dissent and excellence is growing worldwide. "A joy-filled workplace gives people the freedom to use their talents and skills for the benefit of society, without being crushed or controlled by autocratic supervisors" (Bakke, 2013, p. 19). People are people and they desire much of the same things no matter where they live or what language they speak or write.

If workers believe their workplace is conducive to their personal and professional development, they may feel more comfortable coming out of their shells and achieving their full potential. When people's genuine needs aren't addressed, they are more prone to act out of their stress behaviors; this can lead to conflict with others. Bakke (2013) asserted, "We talk a lot about teamwork. But in most of the business world, the people who should be coaching are actually trying to play all the positions [obstructing]" (p. 40). All organizations regardless of their type and size may benefit from understanding what goodwill dissent and finding excellence; and nurturing it may bring to their workplaces. Craig (2014) supposed that "Loyal dissent is usually expressed as carefully thought-out, well-intentioned, usually verbal action designed to help an entire organization or a particular leader perform better and accomplish its mission more successfully... expressed out of genuine concern" (pp. 97-98). Whilst addressing 84 senior cadets majoring in Advanced National Security Studies at the United States Military

Academy in West Point, New York, on April 21, 2008, Defense Secretary Robert M. Gates (as cited in Craig, 2014) said,

> During my time as secretary, I have been impressed by the way the Army's professional journals allow some of our brightest and most innovative officers to critique – sometimes bluntly – the way service does business; to include judgments about senior leadership, both military, and civilian. (p. 101)

If circles such as the army, which are known for a strict chain of command, were talking about the values of goodwill dissent then, why would not the social sector do so now?. In the quotation above, allowing "our brightest and most innovative officers", is the core; leading organizations allow space to hear from those that make the organization tick regardless of their position. Wisdom says tape on the best minds in the organization wherever they exist. Invest in finding them too, and you will. The reality is that best minds are not the preserve of those in the upper echelons of organizational hierarchies.

It is crucial to provide workers with outlets for professional development that encourage them to discover and value the organization's areas of strength, and their own strengths (excellence). It is also recommended to consider the input of marginalized, overlooked and sometimes disregarded stakeholders and staff. Any part of the organization is a fertile ground for new ideas. Organizations need to be open to creation, co-creation, and regeneration from outside in, and from the margins too.

An African saying is – It is an ant that killed an elephant. When I was exploring this wisdom, I was told as tiny as ant is, if it gets in the trunk of an elephant, the elephant is never at easy, it literally can beat its trunk against trees in a bid to have the ant out, but in that process the elephant can seriously hurt itself. This affirms the God-given talent in every person, whether considered tiny or big at work.

TRANSFORMATIONAL SIGNIFICANCE

Organizations window dress when they face the public. Bakke (2013) called it putting "lipstick on a pig" (p. 20). An organization could unleash the potential of its leaders and employees if it uproots a culture that encourages the suppression of talents of individuals and a culture that encourages shaming and blaming, political maneuvering, and stifling. This will result in an ignition of purpose, passion, and motivation (Bakke, 2013). In concurrence, Hamilton said, "Human resource management may extract and exploit workers, whereas human capacity [strengthening] is a distinct paradigm that views workers through a lens of abundance rather than scarcity" (Z. Hamilton, personal communication, April 24, 2022).

The necessity of listening to the voices on the margins has a transformative effect. This voice is often the one that stands out as an anomaly, the one that is peculiar, the one that originates from uncharted territories, and possibly the voice that presents itself in uncharted ways (1 Kings 19:11-15). When the opinions of each worker are heard and considered, and when an organization places a premium on its workers' contentment and satisfaction, the seeds of transformation are planted and given the opportunity to germinate. It is also feasible that happy workers spread their joy to their families and the community around them, creating a transformative ripple effect that will result in citizens who are happier and more productive when they are not at work. It's equally possible that the opposite is true. Employees who are having problems at work may also generate problems for their families and for society. Guven (2011) concluded in his paper "Are happier people better citizens" that people who are content with their lives are more likely to participate in democratic processes (voting, volunteering), value the rule of law, and show compassion toward their fellow citizens.

Below are ideas for giving constructive feedback:

- *Start with a positive statement.* This will help the person feel more receptive to your feedback. For example, you could say something like, "I really appreciate the effort you put into this project."
- *Be specific, and practical.* Focus on the employee's performance, not on their person. After you have pointed out the behavior that you want to change, offer suggestions for how the person can improve. For example, you could say "I think you could improve your writing by using more specific examples."
- *Be timely, and respectful.* Give feedback as soon as possible after the event or behavior that you are commenting on. Offer feedback in a respectful and helpful manner.
- *End on a positive note.* After you have given your feedback, end on a positive note. This will help the person feel more motivated to make the changes you have suggested. For example, you could say something like, "I know you can do this. I am here to help if you need me."

Below are ideas for receiving constructive feedback:

- *Listen actively.* Pay attention to what the person is saying and try to understand their perspective.
- *Ask questions.* If you are not sure what the person is saying, ask them to clarify.

Not all feedback will be positive, and that is fine. It is important to be able to handle both positive and negative feedback in a constructive way. Remember that feedback is a gift, and it can help you improve your work.

- *Be open to feedback.* Be willing to consider the person's feedback and to make changes if necessary. It is easy to take feedback personally, but it's important to remember that feedback is about your work, not about you. Try to focus on the feedback itself and not on how it makes you feel.
- *Appreciate:* Thank the person for their feedback. Let them know that you appreciate their input, time and effort. It is always polite to thank the person who gave you feedback.
- *Act on the feedback:* If you do not take action, people will be less likely to give you feedback in the future. Take some time to reflect on the feedback. What do you agree with? What do you disagree with? How can you use the feedback to improve your work?. If you disagree with feedback, it is important to be respectful and professional. You can always discuss your disagreement with the person who gave you the feedback at a later time.

Chapter 2

FOSTERING GOODWILL DISSENT

A hostile working atmosphere that stifles resourcefulness and talent is a breeding ground for animosity and unhealthy competition. When such an environment crystallizes and hardens, it makes it difficult, if not impossible, to foster productive collaboration. This is where goodwill dissent comes in. Non-conformists are essential to the success of any organization. This is not the kind of individual who would assert that there is only one legitimate method, an improper way (in a straight-jacketed manner), and then the one and only way in which business is conducted. Instead, s/he is open to new ideas and questions, such as "what is the appropriate path for the future?" (Drucker et al., 2008, p. 5). There are advantages to having conflict at the workplace as well as disadvantages. An organization that is peaceful and amicable may very easily be one that is uncreative, stagnant, inflexible, and inattentive to its members' needs (Heffron (as cited in Bolman & Deal, 2017). The presence of conflict poses a threat to the existing quo and piques both attention and curiosity. The presence of conflict may inspire the generation of alternative ideas, approaches and new ways for doing business.

Even though this is not always the case, there is solid reason to believe that many leaders of organizations are typically unaware of the tendency of workers to maintain silence, and if they are aware, they simply turn a blind eye. It is not uncommon for executives and key decision-makers to be unaware of the difficulties and challenges that are experienced by front-line staff.

This failure to perceive silence may be due to the fact that employees are more hands-on, interact regularly at their level, and are positioned where much of the action in a business occurs, whereas leaders generally have more space to think, but are also often isolated from the work floor. It is a problem in workplaces when workers recognize concerns but are unable to offer viable remedies and instead choose to either be quiet, or even worse, learn to accept and live with the problems. Leaders may also have the misconception that people are at liberty to communicate upward, and as a result, they fail to acknowledge the reluctance and anxiety that many employees feel when it comes to upward communication. Many executives with good intentions are unintentionally supporting an authority-ranking social paradigm that some employees enter the workforce expecting to kick in their sixth sense and tread carefully when around those in authority. These dynamics imply that it is necessary to fully understand the elements and conditions that inspire employees to speak up when they have suggestions, information, or opinions.

Employee ideas are crucial drivers of quality decisions and corporate effectiveness, and an important thread in the tapestry of any organization. "Employees are more willing to speak up when they perceive managers as being open and not abusive" (Burris, 2012, p. 851). Management practices can indicate whether speaking up is permitted for all, or only a few. Not speaking up may "shut down creativity and undermine productivity" (Perlow & Williams, 2003, p. 3) and even imperil employees and customers. Morrison (2014) said "If voice is withheld within an organizational context, both performance and employee morale may suffer, so the consequences may be significant" (p. 175). Milliken et al. (2020) asserted that,

> Beyond merely surfacing problems, employees can speak up constructively by also taking steps to mitigate the consequences and prevent the recurrence of those problems by (a) taking action to address the problems and informing managers of these solutions, and (b) offering suggestions to managers about how the problems could be solved. (p. 6)

If employees feel that their places of employment are not safe environments to express themselves, it is possible that they will be reluctant to do so out of fear of receiving unfavorable comments. And certainly, they will talk at the water cooler, when they go out together for coffee, or when they are alone. In my experience, employees are more likely to deploy their voices in the form of goodwill dissent in workplaces that give value to their voice. These are workplaces that trust their employees and allow them to discover their own solutions to obstacles.

From their findings, Unler and Caliskan (2019) concluded that "positive management attitude facilitates supportive and constructive voice (CV) and reduces destructive voice (DESV)" (p. 582). Consistent with this view is the opinion of Perlow and Williams (2003), who believe that criticism in the workplace can provide new and improved ways of accomplishing objectives. Employees who remain silent have the opposite effect; if they lose interest or become uninspired, they may resort to more routine methods of working, thereby decreasing production.

For some managers confronting divergent points of view is trickier than it may appear. It may be unsettling and demanding, and it compels people to act in ways that are outside of their comfort zones. In the same vein some managers believe that more demanding kinds of communication are less productive; as such they are less inclined to endorse them than ideas delivered with a supporting voice. The result is they also end up throwing away the bath water with the baby, killing the message and attacking the messenger. More experiential training is needed on how to leverage on constructive workplace dissent. Leaders, can set the tone for whether or not dissenting perspectives are tolerated in their organizations by delivering unequivocal indications of acceptance, thus allowing workers' voices to be heard.

Employees often prefer to keep their mouths shut out of concern for unpleasant personal and professional repercussions. Even if one is not immediately dismissed, they should brace themselves for marginalization. People worry about losing their jobs. The resulting effect of this is a more submissive and subservient work attitude.

Goodwill dissent is a benefit since it may point to gaps and flaws that need to be addressed. It can provide feedback on ineffective, harmful and unproductive organizational practices and policies, as well as help with appropriate and effective decision-making that considers employers and employees' needs in organizations.

THE AFRICAN CONTEXT

I am an African, born and grew up on the African content. Aside from Africa, I have had the opportunity to live in a few other countries throughout the world. My experience working on the African continent and interacting with African leadership outside of Africa has shown me that African cultural patterns about leadership and management vary from one setting to the next. This is true both within Africa and outside of Africa. Africans belong to different cultures; none of them are homogeneous, but there are common values across the board. In general, Africans are compassionate to others and helpful during times of tragedy and sadness. African cultures often encourage working together to accomplish things by helping and cooperating. The concepts of "ubuntu", collaboration, harmony, and healthy interpersonal relationships are made visible in these behaviors, which are a clear demonstration of those values.

Skepticism and cynicism are common at work, and they can lead to mistrust between employees and managers. Communication perception is one of the motivators for skepticism. The way messages are delivered may prevent collaboration and cooperation. This may be influenced by social and interpersonal cultural norms.

People who grew up in a closed-up culture or family setting are more reticent to speak up, even when they have a good idea in mind. These workers frequently lack self-assurance and the willpower to negotiate with or persuade others, both inside and outside the workplace.

It is also important to be aware of the cultural norms that may influence communication. For example, in some cultures, it is considered rude to disagree and confront someone in public. In these cultures, it is important to find ways to communicate disagreement in a respectful way. This can be done by being honest and transparent, by following through on commitments, and by being supportive of employees. When employees trust their managers, they are more likely to be open to communication and collaboration.

In my experience, one can practice speaking up in safe spaces, such as with friends or family members who they trust. One can also talk to coworkers who allow them to be who they are and can mentor them in their practice and quest to speaking up. Yes, emphatic colleagues, mentors and coaches may help workers to develop their communication skills, especially in workplaces with unhealthy competition, and where supervisors practice management styles that are only work focused, and not work and people.

In some African cultures, the main problems associated with team learning cultural habits seem to be "rigidity, self-centeredness, and defensiveness" (Jetu et al., 2011, p. 65). For instance, in a study on a project team in Ethiopia, results showed that the dominance of one's own view in magnifying their own idea discourages the emergence of constructive ideas and suggestions in project team settings (Jetu et al., 2011). When things go wrong, team members look for someone to blame, save face, or downplay the truth so as not to offend a third party. Concealing information and refusing to face facts may be a source of trouble (Jetu et al., 2011).

The Ethiopian context is not exclusive to this. Even though several African communities are renowned for their members' politeness, selflessness, tolerance, courtesy, cooperation, and for some, lack of direct confrontation, this behavior could be misinterpreted. These beautiful phrases are occasionally used against Africans and may even have negative connotations.

Some African cultures are "high power distance culture(s)," which means they place a high value on submission to those in positions of leadership. The leadership, innovation performance, and learning orientation of organizations and businesses operating on the African continent may be adversely affected by this type of behavior. A high-power distance culture limits employee involvement and weakens their commitment to corporate learning. The result is workplace discontent, and this lowers employee performance and innovation.

Some African cultures have a synchronic meta culture (Trompenaars & Hampden-Turner, 2012). "Synchronic cultures carry their past through the present into the future and will refuse to consider changing unless convinced that their heritage is safe" (Trompenaars & Hampden-Turner, 2012, p. 133). For organizations seeking to implement long-lasting change in highly synchronic cultures, they must take heed of the distant and wealthy era in the civilization of the society they seek to work in. In doing this, change can be drawn from making attempts to recreate some of the greatest glories of the past (Trompenaars & Hampden-Turner, 2012). Leaders ought to learn to contextualize interventions in an incarnational leadership way, rather than blindly importing leadership approaches from elsewhere and expecting them to work in all settings.

Some strategies for goodwill dissent

Goodwill dissent in the workplace relies heavily on techniques that consider employees' personal traits, drives, and motives in addition to their ideas, value systems, experiences, and expertise. Those who have firm convictions should consider what their faith teaches in light of an issue at hand. In such a situation, one hears God's voice. Christians ought to contemplate what Jesus Christ would do in any given situation. Applying one's faith to work and turning it on could be helpful.

According to Hardy, the organization where he works places a strong emphasis on maintaining ethical standards and being transparent in all aspects of business. They were in a scenario where his employer wanted to conduct business in Côte d'Ivoire, and they needed his help. Because of the circumstances, Hardy's company was exploring a deal with a local business in Côte d'Ivoire that was run by a third party to sell telecommunications equipment there. During the due diligence process, Hardy, a lawyer working in the compliance department came across data suggesting that the third party had been accused of multiple instances of fraud and corruption. Although he was uncovering evidence of misconduct, his manager was eager to push the deal through because it appeared to be the only solution, they had available at that moment.

> If we did not decide fast, we were going to lose the third-party. I had to disagree with fostering this agreement. My proposed solution was to put the project on hold. I was also opposed to a complete cancelling of the deal altogether. (J. Hardy, personal communication, November 04, 2022)

This proposed solution allowed the company to buy additional time, resulting in a better deal. Hardy's dissent was based on his expert legal knowledge. The combination of specialized knowledge and its professional application enables employees to have a unique perspective that the organization may not have, equally gainful to an organization.

Goodwill dissent is also effective when individuals seek to complement rather than compete with one another. Employers and employees must be willing to listen, communicate, and act with respect toward others. The red ocean strategy does not help. It can be detrimental to both employees and employers now and in the future.

Zebras: Goodwill dissent works when people seek to...

Goodwill dissent works when people seek to complete each other rather than compete with each other.

Organizations should not be too rigid; they must be open to incorporate ideas that have not been in their mainstream. Organizational leadership should publicly acknowledge and reward such exceptional constructive ideas and performances when they are presented. Acts of goodwill dissent need to permeate the entire organization and be allowed to entrench.

Workers must be concerned about how they measure up to the organization's standards and what it takes to advance their careers. Consideration of an employee's goodwill dissent may spring out of the employee's performance and stature in the organization. It might be claimed that employees who are in good standing with the organization are more likely to be viewed favorably when they voice their disapproval than employees who are not in good standing. "A *good* name [earned by honorable behavior, godly wisdom, moral courage, and personal integrity] is more desirable than great riches; And favor is better than silver and gold". (Proverbs 22:1)

Providing answers, proposals, and options in goodwill dissent is productive, than simply objecting and not presenting any other idea, or alternative. Some of the tactics for goodwill dissent include standing for integrity, exercising due diligence, and considering other possible options before speaking. Employees must dissent with an open mind, not thinking that what they are proposing is the best or will be taken in. Rather than striving to impose one's own views regardless of the consequences, one must intend to achieve mutual benefit for both the employer and the employees. Such an approach moots a better conversation, and interaction.

A further insight shared in one of my conversations is follows.

I experienced a situation in my restaurant business where employees were upset or in disagreement about how tips were being distributed. Some felt certain employees were allowed to keep too large of a percentage of tips than acceptable instead of sharing them with others. The employees who were upset brought it to my attention but not in constructive ways. One employee challenged my competence and knowledge and resigned because we ultimately did not change the structure as we felt it was appropriate, and no better ideas were presented. The disagreement culminated during a work shift when customers were present too. It was not good timing. The other employee stayed with us and later benefited from a different incentive plan we implemented, when revenue increased, that involved bonuses instead of sharing tips. (G. Kokeke, personal communication, December 30, 2022)

Desta proffered another strategy as follows.

When dissenting or when disagreeing with one's supervisor, it is very important to understand the environment and the timing for such dissent, and also not to do it in a humiliating manner, and overly criticize someone's position or advancement. I simply think one needs to create an environment that is suitable for the person that you are engaging to make your dissent. The timing and the strategy you will use are all important. Sometimes it is all about the best timing and best strategy to dissent constructively. You certainly are not going to present your helpful suggestions in the midst of your manager's fury, are you? (F. Desta, personal communication, November 4, 2022)

Ideal Workplace in terms of Goodwill Dissent

The following is a depiction of an ideal workplace in terms of goodwill dissent, as shared by some of the interviewees.

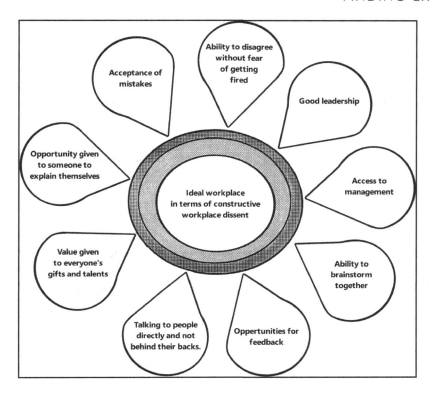

An interviewee said an ideal workplace in terms of goodwill dissent is "is a place where people can speak their mind, and an environment that allows and facilitates doing things differently but towards a common goal." Another interviewee shared that a workplace embodying goodwill dissent resolves challenges by finding solutions together and accords an equal chance to employees to contribute.

The following illustration by Kudzai touched on a number of aspects in relation to rewarding good behavior and excellence.

A thought that comes to mind is that I love dogs. Therefore, I have two dogs at home. I have had to train them. I have so much of a passion for these animals, so I have gone to puppy school. They invite you to puppy school as if they are training the puppy, but they are actually training the handler. Therefore, they say reward good behavior. If you always reward good behavior, the dog will learn and know that this is good. If it does something bad or maybe you were playing, and it starts to bite then play stops. This way the dog learns to know that biting is not the right thing to do. On the other hand, before I went to puppy school, I used to think the best way to train a dog when it does something bad was to hit it. Rather it turns out that hitting the dog causes it to regress and it cultivates behavior that you do not want, so no corporal punishment for the dog. My ideal is that there is a celebration for constructive dissent which is outright and public; and secondly, there is clear communication that we will not punish for disagreeing but also that we will not celebrate destructive dissent. (M. Kudzai, personal communication, December 05, 2022)

Some key informants shared that ideal workplaces are places where employees at the low grades feel that they can speak up, and where they are made to feel that they are important for the achievement of an organizations' mission.

If they feel that they are important towards the big goals of the organization, if they feel they are contributors - that is one of my dreams. On the other hand, if the leadership and management feel that everybody contributes towards the achievement of the goals of the organization like in systems thinking, where every part in the system is important. This is ideal. (F. Yohannes, personal communication, December 05, 2022)

The most successful workplaces foster open communication between management and staff. In an ideal workplace, leadership is reliable and does not go back on its word; they say what they mean and do what they say. Dejen noted that "When employers and employees dissent in the workplace, it is more powerful to demonstrate the behavior one is proposing - many people follow our life, our behavior more than our speech (R. Dejen, personal communication, December 09, 2022). In relation to Dejen's view, Netsanet said, "Employees can dissent constructively when they demonstrate love and compassion in their dissent. This way they can win the hearts of other employees and employers" (A. Netsanet, personal communication, November 29, 2022).

It is feasible to encourage goodwill dissent. Conflict is not always negative. What sets apart effective leaders is how they deal with conflict. Organizations only remain competitive through healthy competition. "Iron sharpens iron, and one man sharpens another" (Proverb 27:17). Allowing for the expression of differing points of view is actually beneficial to the success of businesses. Dissent that is motivated by goodwill creates innovations and results that otherwise would not be experienced. When workers are exposed to multiple compelling examples of goodwill dissent, the likelihood that they will gravitate toward it increases. Both employers and employees need to voice their disagreements in a way that's beneficial while maintaining the conviction that the system works. Goodwill dissent is not a figment of imagination. It is feasible.

Here I would like to emphasize the point that finding Excellence in employees by appreciating and expressing gratitude for the good they do, and the talents they exhibit to the organization demonstrably adds value. It generates more goodwill dissent.

Eskedar shared about a homeless person who resided outside the compound of a premise, where a church-related development organization she worked for had its headquarters. Most of the employees in that compound were familiar with this homeless individual. The individual was filthy. He had mental illness concerns as well. The organization's policy was to be cautious of such people, while also avoiding bringing them into the property as much as possible. It was an unwritten rule, but customary.

On the day in question, Eskedar arrived at the workplace and noticed the homeless person in distress at the gate. The first notion that came to mind was not to bring the person into the compound, but on second thought, Eskedar does. Others saw that and were bothered. Eskedar spent two hours of work time with this person helping him. She later gave the little money she had to buy food. Then Eskedar stayed behind at work for two hours at the end of the day to finish reports that were due. Her boss, who witnessed the entire scene, was unimpressed. That homeless person came looking for Eskedar five years later. God had been gracious to the homeless person, and he was now working in another province of the country. Eskedar's actions later influenced the organization's policy to urge employees to assess situations before shutting them out.

Eskeder's sharing triggered the following story.

> It reminds me of a church I helped start in South Dakota that met in a reclaimed warehouse. We called it Church at the Warehouse. Many people who were currently or had in the past dealt with addiction and who had been in treatment, jail and prison gathered for worship and to share a meal once each week, about 125 people. One of the associate pastors who had been a Christian for a few years and had served as a deacon at another church, actually used to sleep outside that warehouse building years earlier when he was active in his addiction. I did not know this until one time during a conversation when he shared it. We all praised God. I do not think he knew how special his transformation and his story was until he shared it, and people responded. (Z. Hamilton, personal communication, December 30, 2022)

Biruk shared a story in the context of organization X, which works in some of the fragile states. Ordinarily, their staff experience traumatic situations because of the insecure and hostile environments in which they operate. The normal practice in organization X is to have pastoral care support. In most cases, pastoral support is provided by staff based in organization X's head office who would be brought to the field to help employees working in complex emergency relief situations. Whilst there is nothing bad about that approach, Biruk's motivation for constructive workplace dissent was based on the cultural context and knowledge of what staff experience in his county which was also his duty station. Biruk's dissent was the conviction that it would be important for organization X to have pastoral care done by people who are closer to the context and can continue one-on-one or a series of engagements where needed. This approach would be a departure from the norm. Biruk's ideas had not been done elsewhere in the field offices of organization X. It was a difficult discussion to moot. However, the decision to have pastoral care done by the people closer to the context is something that was later adopted as policy in Biruk's organization. Now several countries where Biruk's organization works are trying to make sure that pastoral care support is as local as possible and close to the context in which it is supposed to be provided. "When one dissents out of goodwill the truth is that sometimes you do not know how that is going to be received by your supervisors if not by the organization as a whole" (T. Biruk, personal communication, October 12, 2022).

Biruk's sharing is a great example of asset-based community development (ABCD), which can be summarized by the principle that people closest to the problem have the best solutions, if organizations only ask and trust them, and encourage them to trust themselves. Biruk's sharing drives home the metaphor of a pastor being a shepherd who cares for a flock and requires them to be present with the flock more than they are away. "My sheep hear my voice, and I know them, and they follow me. I give them eternal life, and they will never perish, and no one will snatch them out of my hand" (John 10:27-28).

Afework shared a story from one of the regions of Ethiopia whereby the culture there is that men are the ones who receive humanitarian assistance on behalf of the family - as heads of the family. Afework's organization was in one of the flood-stricken regions to provide cash distributions to families and individuals in the flood-affected communities. Afework started having conversations with the community leaders as well as the religious leaders in the region with the intention and interest of Afework's organization to have women receive the cash instead of men. Practically, if the men collected the cash, it felt obvious that they would spend the money on buying *khat*. *Khat* is green leaves that act as a stimulant, which most men in some regions of Ethiopia eat. It is also accessible in the corner shops of urban centres like Addis Ababa, and others (then). Through long discussions with the government representatives, community leaders, and religious leaders, Afework's organization influencing skills finally led to having 75% percentage of the cash being collected by women and 25% by men. Afework said

> It is risky bringing in such conversations and changes in a community that is used to living differently. But we were determined. We stood for what we believed was right. However, organizations need to be vigilant in following through with monitoring the implementation of such interventions in a very strong way to see if the change is bringing the transformation it is intended,

and not disharmony in the families. (L. Afework, personal communication, November 19, 2022)

On a similar note, Zinaye shared that,

> I constantly consider what is consistent with my values system, such as what would benefit the people I serve in the community, their needs, my coworkers, and humankind as a whole. This is what motivates my dissent. When I must dissent, it must not be about me, but for others and, of course, God.
> (G. Zinaye, personal communication, November 14, 2022)

When Felomain was working in organization Y, she was invited to a meeting with the largest donors to her country, which was organized by the government's social welfare department. When the speaker indicated that they were going to provide in-kind gifts and donations through three- to six-month intervention projects, Felomain was the only one who openly objected, even though her supervisor might not have approved. There were approximately 50 nongovernmental organizations there in the room. Felomain said that she responded,

> Listen, if you want to turn us into poor communities by continuing to give us little gifts for short periods of time, rather than building the communities by empowering them, we do not welcome these forms of donations. Communities do not require any further in-kind gifts, or three- or six-month projects that terminate with the end of distribution of your help. Instead, we require something tangible to encourage and empower people in our communities. Teach me to fish, but do not give me fish always. (N. Felomain, personal communication, November 14, 2022)

Felomain says her conviction and audacity astonished the meeting's convenor, including her supervisor. Through her dissent on that day, she felt that she had represented the real needs of her community.

> The good that resulted from my intervention was that the approaches to donor help began to change, from addressing short term needs only to embrace projects that would address long term needs too. (N. Felomain, personal communication, November 14, 2022)

SOME KEY TAKEAWAYS

Goodwill dissent helps organizations to think outside the box, to be creative, and to be innovative.

Faith and belief:

Faith and one's belief system is one key driving factor for goodwill dissent in the workplace. Though culture and upbringing has a major role in guiding and determining when and where employees could dissent with goodwill, faith comes in too. Organizations would be more encouraged to promote goodwill dissent if their leaders believed in it, or the dominant belief system among the leaders' religion promoted it, or if a firm or public service institution is led by a person with a strong religious belief system that value others' voices.

For many people, their faith is a source of strength and conviction, and it can give them the courage to speak up when they perceive something to be wrong. Additionally, many faith traditions emphasize the importance of speaking out against injustice and oppression, which can lead people to feel a moral obligation to dissent constructively.

Conviction and motive:

There are circumstances when employees engage in goodwill dissent because they believe certain situations necessitate it. It is a moral obligation for people to speak up when they perceive things to be not going in the right direction. Conviction and motive are two important factors that can influence whether an employee will engage in goodwill dissent. Conviction refers to the employee's belief that the situation is wrong and needs to be changed, while motive refers to the employee's reason for speaking up. Employees who are more convicted about a situation are more likely to speak up, and believe that it is the right thing to do, even if it is not the easy thing to do. Also employees who are motivated by a desire to improve the situation are more likely to speak up. They are also more likely to be constructive in their words and conduct, and to propose solutions to a problem. When employees' motives are good, they are more likely to dissent with goodwill.

Specialized and expertise knowledge:

Employees with specialized knowledge in their fields of work or contexts may have more confidence to dissent constructively because of their possession of specialized knowledge. Examples from the stories shared by interviewees were of advisors, lawyers, organizational development experts, internal auditors, compliance specialists, programme evaluators, senior advisors, among others. From their education, experiences, and expertise knowledge, they may offer valuable insights and solutions. They are usually perceived to dissent out of goodwill.

When done effectively, dissent can help to improve organizations and make them more effective.

Some ideas for employees with specialized knowledge who want to dissent constructively:

- *Do your research.* Make sure you have a good understanding of the issue before you dissent.
- *Be respectful.* Even if you disagree with someone and have expertise knowledge, there is no need to be rude or condescending.
- *Be specific.* Do not just say "I disagree." Explain why you disagree and offer suggestions for how things could be done differently.
- *Be open to feedback.* Be willing to listen to other people's perspectives and to consider their ideas.
- *Be willing to compromise.* Do not expect to always get your way. Be willing to give and take in order to reach a solution that everyone can agree on.

Below are just a few examples of how employees with specialized knowledge have dissented constructively.

- An advisor to a government agency dissented from a proposal to cut funding for a program that she believed was essential. She provided evidence that the program was effective and that cutting funding would have negative consequences. The agency ultimately decided to keep funding the program.
- A lawyer at a law firm dissented from a decision to represent a client that he believed was guilty. He explained his concerns to his colleagues and ultimately convinced them to withdraw from the case.
- An organizational development expert at a nonprofit organization dissented from a proposal to change the organization's structure. She argued that the change would be disruptive and that it would not improve the organization's effectiveness. The organization ultimately decided not to make the change.
- An internal auditor at a company dissented from a decision to approve a large investment. She raised concerns about the risks of the investment and ultimately convinced the company to reject it.
- A compliance specialist at a bank dissented from a decision to approve a loan to a high-risk borrower. He argued that the loan was not in the bank's best interest and that it would violate the bank's lending policies. The bank ultimately decided not to make the loan.
- A program evaluator at a government agency dissented from a report that he believed was inaccurate and misleading. He provided evidence to support his concerns and ultimately convinced the agency to revise the report.

- A senior advisor to a government official dissented from a decision to make a major policy change. She argued that the change would be harmful and that it would not achieve the government's objectives. The government official ultimately decided not to make the change.

Best interests of the organization:

Employees' dissent must be in the best interest of the organization. Dissent must be aimed at eliminating bottlenecks that prevent employees from meeting their obligations and performing to their full potential. Employees with a track record of dissenting constructively by giving suggestions that are in line with the mission and goals of the organization are likely to attract more attention.

It is important for employees to understand the difference between constructive and destructive dissent. Constructive dissent is aimed at improving the organization, while destructive dissent is aimed at undermining it.

Alternatives:

Providing solutions, recommendations, and options when dissenting is one of the best approaches. This approach is in contrast to simply objecting without presenting other ideas or pointing to the right way. However, when employees perceive something to be not right, and they do not have an alternative, it is still best to speak up with an intention that a possible solution may be found together through consultation and discussion. Let your manager or colleagues know that you are concerned about the issue, and ask if there is anything you can do to help. Be open to discussing the issue and trying to find a solution together. Sometimes, the best outcome is simply to get the issue on the table and to start a conversation about it. If one can do that, they have already made a valuable contribution.

Dissent with an open mind:

Employees must dissent with an open mind, not thinking that what they are proposing is the best or will be taken in. Rather than striving to impose one's own views regardless of the circumstances, one must intend to achieve mutual benefit for both employers and employees. This moots a better conversation, and interaction. This means that one is willing to listen to other perspectives and to consider their ideas. When employees dissent with an open mind, they are more likely to have a productive conversation with supervisors or colleagues.

Timing and strategy: When dissenting, it is important to grasp the atmosphere and the moment that is amiable for such dissent, but also the choice of language. It is important to do it in a manner that is not embarrassing and to refrain from unnecessarily criticizing others viewpoints. Employees need to be aware that for the issue at hand, it may not be the first time that a particular issue is being discussed, and it might be helpful to wait until one has had a chance to gather more information or to develop their own ideas.

Chapter 3

HUMAN FLOURISHING

Human flourishing may be related to Bakke's Joy at work model which is a model premised on his "passion... to make work exciting, rewarding, stimulating and enjoyable" (p. 13). Bakke (2005) postulated that workers "want a chance to meet the needs of their families while doing something useful to society" (p. 25) and meeting a higher purpose. In not just creating shareholder value, Bakke (2005) asserted that "The principal goal or purpose of the company is stewarding its resources to serve society in an economical manner... The primary evaluation criterion is economic performance related to creating shareholder value" (p. 25). The Joy at Work model takes into account each employee's unique abilities. Employees are allowed to make decisions and key choices on their work portfolios, including those related to budgets - they simply need to seek advice when needed, but not clearance as such from supervisors (Bakke, 2013). Related to self-accountability is the fact that performance appraisals would hitch upon more self-evaluation supported by feedback from supervisors and colleagues. Leaders should take a servant leadership approach in their relationship to their subordinates, adopting an attitude of mentorship, coaching, teaching, and cheerleading, while promoting self-accountability. Leadership that is astute recognizes that they already have the workforce capacity that the company needs to prosper, unless the recruitment process had been flawed or simply missed the mark. Competent leaders develop the talent of those they already employ.

Bakke (2005) advanced that, what makes a workplace joyful is when organizations create spaces that allow employees to use their talents and skills for the greater good, much as players on a team do not have to ask the coach if they should score right now, when the opportunity arises.

Happiness has attracted the attention of philosophers since the dawn of written history (McMahon, 2006, as cited in Fischer, 2010, p. 384). The birth of positive psychology (Seligman et al, 2005) legitimized the emphasis on happiness and other positive states over the previously dominant disease paradigm, which disproportionately focused on illness, and other unpleasant experiences and effects.

Joy at work vitalizes organizations, and employees. It is a necessity. The 2016 survey by the Deloitte Center for the Edge (2013), of 3,159 full-time American workers, revealed that "only 13 percent of respondents exhibited all three attributes of worker passion: commitment to domain, questing, and connecting dispositions" (p. 22). This finding equates to a larger portion of employees who are unhappy, less passionate, and less motivated at work. Naber (2007), an industrial and organizational psychologist, and data scientist revealed that "the average person will spend 90,000 hours at work over a lifetime" (para. 1). If people spend such a large portion of their lives at work, should not human flourishing be a critical facet for finding purpose and achieving organizational missions?

Haile thought that emotional wellbeing matters in the workplace, "Unless that workplace is psychologically humane employees will not flourish. If employees are emotionally negatively affected in the workplace, their productivity is affected" (E. Haille, personal communication, December 09, 2022. In concurrence Dejen said "psychological safety helps to increase productivity, to increase relationships, and to achieve happiness at work (R. Dejen, personal communication, December 09, 2022). People are unique - they are one of a kind. Recognizing and putting such distinctiveness at the center of an individual's potential can help workers grow and thrive. Handy (1999, as cited in James, 2012) proffered,

> I reckon that our organizations could do with a deal more loving, a bit more forgiveness and a lot more faith in other people. Such things, however, in organizations are only possible if we feel we are in the grip of something bigger than ourselves. (p. 16)

Organizations could also be more supportive.

> But Moses' hands grew weary, so they took a stone and put it under him, and he sat on it, while Aaron and Hur held up his hands, one on one side, and the other on the other side. So his hands were steady until the going down of the sun. (Exodus 17:12)

Critics of joy at work are uninterested. Some even think it is a nebulous concept. Spicer and Cederström (2015) argued that it is merely an attractive notion on paper, "the aesthetic part," and nothing more. The authors argued that it is flimsy to ignore the crux of the workplace - the disputes and politics that smother "the ideological part." Critics also believe that happiness occurs naturally and that attempting to create it will be futile (Spicer & Cederström, 2015). Bauer (2015), in a survey of British supermarkets, found no correlation between joy at work and corporate productivity. In fact, the survey discovered that the more miserable the employees were the better the profits. Hamilton (2022) said, "This is fascinating. I saw this firsthand in my restaurant. The less employees we have and more overworked a small group of employees are, the more profit we have" (Z. Hamilton, personal communication, July 18, 2022). It is a paradox.

Nonetheless, I strongly believe that human flourishing, and the Joy at Work model premised on Bakke's "passion… to make work exciting, rewarding, stimulating and enjoyable" (Bakke, 2013, p. 13) is profound. Meeting work targets and high profits when one is waning away, and disintegrating inside – mentally, emotionally, and spiritually is the paradox. Calming on the surface and paddling like the dickens underneath is certainly killing. Winning with dignity and emotional well-being is ideal. Employers and employees must meet each other halfway point. In my 26 years of work experience, I have counseled co-workers who have felt the grinding teeth of what they had described as the inhumane part of what organizations can do, or what humans can do to other humans – they have felt chewed up and spit. And of course, they had to pick their pieces and move on. While some of them went on to achieve remarkable success, others plummeted to even below their previous circumstances.

The Joy at work model allows space for employees to make major decisions. When uncertain, employees are free to sound board their coworkers, peers and supervisors for advice. This position relates to the requirement for employees to have complete control over their portfolios, in ways that are both empowering and prudent. Bakke (2013) goes on to say that most employees are willing to take full responsibility for their actions if given the freedom to do so in a productive (but not irresponsible) manner. This approach certainly acknowledges that all people falter, no one is perfect; and certainly, people will make mistakes; it is through learning from these mistakes that workers master their jobs and improve. I would argue that making and learning from mistakes is part of climbing and progressing on the ladder of success.

It is possible to create happy workplaces. When Dennis W. Bakke started the Applied Energy Services Corporation (AES), he insisted on the belief that work should be fun and joyful. Bakke (2005) explained

> I was CEO of AES, an energy company that by 2002 had plants in 31 countries, $8.6 billion in revenue, $33, 7 billion in assets, and 40,000 AES people. In a dozen years of operations, we had developed a highly unconventional workplace culture [Joy at Work] and also achieved enviable financial results. (p. 15)

The Joy at Work concept encourages individuals to evaluate their own performance from all angles, including hearing from their superiors and peers. If an employer takes a step back during the performance review process, they will be more capable of seeing the bigger picture of an employee's strengths and areas that need growth. The strengths of employees not only help leaders and managers to uncover greatness, but also helps them to identify the uniqueness, purpose, and worth in others, as well as to discover what makes individual employees tick.

Some ideas on cascading human flourishing in the workplace.

- **Creating a positive work environment:** A positive work environment is one that is supportive, encouraging, and respectful. It is a place where employees feel valued and appreciated.
- **Providing opportunities for learning and development:** Employees need opportunities to learn and grow in order to flourish. Organizations can provide these opportunities through training, development programs, and mentoring.
- **Encouraging employees to take care of themselves:** Employees need to take care of their physical, emotional, and social well-being in order to flourish. Organizations can encourage employees to do this by providing tea/coffee breaks, offering flexible work arrangements, promoting employee wellness programs and others.
- **Creating a sense of community:** Employees need to feel connected to their colleagues and to the organization. Organizations can create a sense of community by providing opportunities for employees to socialize, celebrate successes, and support each other.
- **Providing opportunities for employees to make a difference:** Employees need to feel like they are making a difference in the world. Organizations can provide these opportunities by giving employees opportunities to volunteer, donate to charity, or work on projects that have a positive impact on society.

Chapter 4

EMOTIONAL WELL BEING

According to the Centre for Creative Leadership (n.d.), psychological safety is

> a common conviction held by members of a team that others on the team would not disgrace, reject, or punish you for speaking up... [this] doesn't imply that everyone is always polite. It means you embrace controversy and speak up, confident in the knowledge that your team has your back, and you have theirs. When people are afraid to talk about efforts that aren't working, the organization isn't prepared to avoid failure. (Centre for Creative Leadership, n.d.)

Delizonna (2017) advanced that "Studies show that psychological safety allows for moderate risk-taking, speaking your mind, creativity, and sticking your neck out without fear of having it cut off - just the types of behavior that lead to market breakthroughs" (para. 1). Emotional wellbeing gives confidence to people in organizations to express themselves with goodwill dissent, thereby allowing them to flourish at work.

According to Clark (2021), Edgar Schein and Warren Bennis of the Massachusetts Institute of Technology first introduced the concept of psychological safety to academic research in 1965. They defined it as a climate in which people feel free to speak up without fear of being judged by their superiors, and other staff.

Admitting mistakes, providing constructive criticism of a project, and speaking honestly, especially about fears, while keeping the best interests of the organization and its stakeholders in mind, are all ways to make the workplace more hospitable. Without any ulterior motives; honesty, openness, truthfulness, and sincerity flourish in psychologically secure work environments. An organizational culture that promotes unimpeded information flow and candor among employees and leaders may serve as an early warning to challenges and bottlenecks; however, fear of reprisals is the main obstacle to candor, so addressing it improves long-term shareholder value. Edmondson (2020) affirmed that psychological safety is not a license to slack off, gripe, or overshare. When sharing work-related content, people should remain responsible and courteous (Edmondson, 2020). Edmondson further asserted that it is important to note that psychological safety is not the goal, but excellence in the pursuit of the organization's mission is.

> A nurse on a night shift in a busy urban hospital noticed that the dosage for a particular patient seems a bit high. Believingly she considers calling the doctor at home to check the order. She immediately recalls the discouraging comment about her abilities last time she called him at home [and stops] … quite far from the urban hospital a young pilot in a military training flight notices that his senior officer might have made a crucial misjudgment, he lets the moment go by. (Edmondson, 2019)

These tragic occurrences illustrate the prevalence of silence in the workplace. The catastrophic situations in the preceding quote could have been avoided if the employees involved had prior positive experiences with their voice at work.

Emotional wellbeing matters. Workers are expected to be themselves and have the ability as well as the self-assurance to express their feelings of joy, disappointment, and disagreement at any given time. Organizations have a responsibility to make room for employees' voices to be heard and to provide them with opportunities to do so. Employees are more likely to raise issues in the workplace if they feel they may do so in an atmosphere of psychological safety. Employees are more motivated to achieve and work to enable the company to succeed in a way that is consistent with its mission and vision when they feel psychologically safe. This is intriguing because it demonstrates that workers who experience high levels of psychological safety are better able to act autonomously in the workplace. This is despite the presumption that people need to be motivated to work, that they do not have personal ambitions, and they are not inspired to achieve work objectives. Employees must be trusted to establish their own self-drive, and independence.

Dream Workplace with Regards to Psychological Safety

A workplace free from discrimination and where mental health is prioritized is ideal. Employers need to allow for breathers/gaps between work schedules to allow workers to unwind. Lunch breaks help so are annual leave days, and spaces for rest and recuperation after working in harsh conditions. Ideal psychologically safe workplaces value accountability over leadership's enthusiasm to criticize everyone for a mistake made by one or a group of people. The person who needs to be corrected must be the one to get correction. Employees need to develop skills to be less sensitive and quickly offended to allow others to speak the truth and be sincere. Employees need to be on the lookout for one another. Employers must allow criticism and receive it without antagonism. This is not to say sanctioning unsatisfactory performance or behavior must not happen but giving warnings to staff before being let go must be considered.

Employees ought to be free to be their true selves. Employers must consider giving them autonomy to exercise their God-given talents, skills, and knowledge without micromanaging. Work expectations need to be realistic and clearly communicated.

Emotional wellbeing helps in having a good relationship with God. When an employee is experiencing emotional insecurity, one is likely to have a challenging relationship not only with other employees, but also with God.

Employers need not take employees by surprise on key decisions that affect their possibility to continue in the organization. There has to be certainty always. Psychologically safe places value relationships, seek to strengthen relationships, and strive to build even stronger ones.

Dawit mentioned that

> One ideal of a psychological workplace is where employees and employers have the openness to be vulnerable and being accepted as they are. In such spaces, brave and honest communication is done with love, compassion, and with integrity (F. Dawit, personal communication, November 29, 2022).

Desta shared that

> In a big institution such as ours, counselling must be made part of ministry to the workers. This may be achieved by having a staff counsellor or where staff are facilitated to have access to counselling services outside the work environment. (L. Desta, personal communication, October 15, 2022)

Zeni said psychosocially safe workplaces employ "equitable standards of employment and conditions for all staff. These are places that recognize and acknowledge staff when they meet organizational objectives." (T. Zeni, personal communication, September 09, 2022)

Employees must be encouraged to speak the truth always. Only the truth will stand forever. Christ Jesus spoke the truth. Another example of standing for truth is Daniel in the furnace and the lion's den with Shadrach, Meshack, and Abednego. They remained steadfast, and the Lord God was with them (Daniel 3:8-25).

Employees need to be assured that there will be no retaliation or measures taken against them which will have adverse consequences for them in the workplace now, and their future; be it their career, demeanor, or status. Organizations must inculcate a speak-up culture. Moreover, it is vital for employers to be available, and accessible emotionally; to be there to listen, acknowledge, and encourage.

Solomon said,

> Psychological safety matters because leaders have to be open to our teams, taking their input, encouraging them and rewarding hard work. It is usually not easy for employees to express their ideas, but organizations may do well by facilitating employees to speak up. (R. Solomon, personal communication, October 28, 2022)

Bemnet shared that employers must acknowledge and reward meaningful contributions from employees and thank them with sincerity. She also shared that employers ought to "practice active listening and be available emotionally to support staff. More important, leaders must not lose their cool in front of staff, because that undermines confidence and trust from employees" (T. Bemnet, personal communication, October 28, 2022).

Further Bethlehem said,

> Psychological safety is important especially for lower-level staff and female workers, where culture and capacity in knowledge and confidence are mostly militating against their motivation and power to stand up and speak for themselves. (F. Bethlehem, personal communication, October 28, 2022)

Bethlehem further opined that in patriarchal societies, men feel more comfortable in the workplace because the workplace creates a platform for them to flourish. When employees sense a lack of psychological safety in the workplace,

> they will begin to create parallel communities, built around their own fears. When people are vulnerable, organizations can be volatile, especially where there is nothing that binds employees together. Where there is fear, situations may also be volatile. Psychological safety helps to bring people together. (M. Kudzai, personal communication, December 09, 2022)

SOME KEY TAKEAWAYS

Emotional wellbeing is important in the workplace.

Relationship with God:

The relationship that one has with God can provide love, support, and guidance. When employees are emotionally healthy, they are better able to connect with God and to dissent constructively. When employees are emotionally healthy, they are more likely to hear God's voice and to follow His leading. This can help them to make better workplace decisions and personal decisions.

Speak the truth with love:

In Ephesians 4:15, the Bible instructs to "speak the truth in love." This means that Christ's followers must be honest with each other, even when it is difficult. Employees and employers should always speak with love and compassion, even when they are disagreeing. In John 8:32, Jesus says, "You will know the truth, and the truth will set you free." This means that employees and employees can make choices that are based on truth, rather than on fear or ignorance. When employees feel like they can trust their managers, they are more likely to be honest with them, which can lead to better decision-making and problem-solving.

Assure no retaliation:

It is important to assure employees that they will not face retaliation for reporting wrongdoing or for engaging in protected activity. Employees must have a process in place for employees to report retaliation and to investigate and address any complaints made.

This can help to identify and address problems early on. However, allowing goodwill dissent at work does not mean that employees can say whatever they want. Employees still have to be respectful of their colleagues and their managers.

Listen, acknowledge, encourage, and assist emotionally:

Employers should be available emotionally for their employees and be there to listen, acknowledge, and encourage them. This means being open to hearing their concerns, providing support, and offering guidance. It also means understanding and being compassionate.

Support voices from the periphery:

Innovation can start from any part of the organization including the edges. Employers must not ignore voices from the periphery because they can provide valuable insights and perspectives. Lower-level personnel may have a better understanding of the day-to-day operations of an organization at their level, while female workers and young workers may have different perspectives on workplace culture. Additionally, employees with less experience, exposure, or expertise may still have valuable ideas too. When employers consider voices from the periphery, they are more likely to make decisions that are well-rounded.

Chapter 5

FINDING EXCELLENCE

Finding excellence seeks the best in people, their organizations, and the environment around them by consciously discovering what gives life to an employee, to an organization or a community and finding what makes an organization productive and capable. Finding excellence discovers the positives in organizations and the people in them and seeks to anchor its work on giving value in areas where people excel as opposed to negativity, criticisms, and complaints only.

> Finally, believers, whatever is true, whatever is honorable *and* worthy of respect, whatever is right *and* confirmed by God's word, whatever is pure *and* wholesome, whatever is lovely *and* brings peace, whatever is admirable *and* of good repute; if there is **any excellence,** if there is anything worthy of praise, think *continually* on these things [center your mind on them, and implant them in your heart]. The things which you have learned and received and heard and seen in me, practice these things [in daily life], and the God [who is the source] of peace *and* well-being will be with you. (Philippians 4:8-9)

finding Excellence plants seeds of gratitude for the work done by employers and employees. This ignites workers intellectual curiosity and ingenuity, thereby encouraging dreaming and designing homegrown destinies. In finding Excellence, organizations explore and allow their staff to generate feedback, and occasionally dialogue, by asking and appreciating them in the hope of obtaining knowledge that would help employees to become more aware of their strengths and potential. This may be likened to the Appreciative Inquiry (AI) approach which:

> assumes that every organization and community has many untapped and rich accounts of the positive - what people talk about as past, present, and future

capacities, or the positive core. AI links the knowledge and energy of this core directly to an organization or a community's change agenda, and changes never thought possible are suddenly and democratically [made possible]. (Cooperrider & Whitney, 2005, p. 8)

Instead, Christ's words challenge humanity to resist by doing good. finding Excellence feels like providing light to darkness, like Jesus Christ said, no more "An eye for an eye and a tooth for a tooth.' But I say to you, do not resist the one who is evil" (Matthew 5:38-42). By focusing on finding Excellence in the qualities of employees, employers help to springboard curiosity, thereby propelling employees to seeking a higher calling, which surpass their current good performance.

In seeking to find excellence, I sought to hear stories of goodwill dissent based on the lived experiences of employers and employees in workplaces. Motivations and intentions for goodwill dissent in the workplace varied. For some it was out of conviction that the situation at hand required them to operate outside the norm with no intention of causing harm to employees or the employer. Their motivation was rather to edify processes in their organizations by telling the truth. In telling the truth some key employees quoted "So Jesus said to the Jews who had believed him, 'If you abide in my word, you are truly my disciples, and you will know the truth, and the truth will set you free" (John 8:31-32).

EHIP Framework for Flourishing Employee Talents

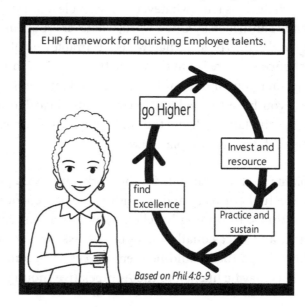

EHIP framework for flourishing Employee talents.

go Higher

Invest and resource

find Excellence

Practice and sustain

Based on Phil 4:8-9

find Excellence:

In finding excellence, organizations acknowledge and celebrate the excellence they see in their employees. finding Excellence must be genuine and publicly celebrated. Employers must publicly praise and privately correct people. When organizations or firms achieve greatness, or if they may have achieved an award, they must reward and recognize their employees' contributions. Employers and employees may do well in dwelling on "whatever is true, whatever is honorable, whatever is just, whatever is pure, whatever is lovely, whatever is commendable… [and] anything worthy of praise" (Philippians 4:8-9).

Go Higher:

The proper response to achievement is not to rest easy in one's excellence now but to push oneself to new heights, to be creative, curious and ambitious. Employers and employees might do what futurists do and look to the years ahead to start painting the vision of the future they need based on the excellence of today. Employers and employees require downtime for rejuvenation and celebration, but they must also keep their eyes on the future they hope to create by visioning and picturing it. Today's excellences must help to lay the foundations for what the future is calling to - the greater destiny God is calling people to.

Invest and resource:

Investing means putting pillars in place to support the futuristic vision. It's figuring out what anchor will work best and how deep you need to dig in order to sustain that future vision. This higher calling needs to be resourced with both human and financial capital, and a spiritual calling too. What do leaders put in place today to help the organization walk towards that vision, but also what resources would be needed to sustain that future when organizations reach there? A lot of forecasting needs to be done. Spaces then need to be created to journey that path. This creation of spaces might be through an innovation space in an organization. Les Brown once said,

> The graveyard is the richest place on earth, because it is here that you will find all the hopes and dreams that were never fulfilled, the books that were never written, the songs that were never sung, the inventions that were never shared, the cures that were never discovered, all because someone [did not invest in them]. (Brown, n.d.)

Practice & sustain: Practicing and sustaining is what breathes life to organizational and individual plans. The previous quotation from Les Brown applies here too. It is only when employers and employees genuinely take out fear from workplaces that goodwill dissent, emotional wellbeing, and joy at work begins to crystallize and permeate across an organization.

Visions only have value if they are put into action and kept alive throughout time. A lion on paper remains a lion on paper, it is never real.

Employers and employees may use the EHIP framework for flourishing employee talents [see page 32]. The EHIP framework was inspired by the following biblical Scripture.

Finally, [a]believers, whatever is true, whatever is honorable *and* worthy of respect, whatever is right *and* confirmed by God's word, whatever is pure *and* wholesome, whatever is lovely *and* brings peace, whatever is admirable *and* of good repute; if there is **any excellence,** if there is anything worthy of praise, think *continually* on these things [center your mind on them, and implant them in your heart]. [9] The things which you have learned and received and heard and seen in me, practice these things [in daily life], and the God [who is the source] of peace *and* well-being will be with you. (Philippians 4:8-9)

Chapter 6

HIGHER CALLING

HIGHER CALLING

The following depicts the responses from the encounters I had with interviewees to the question "What is their aspiration of a workplace that makes them happy?"

What Makes Employees Happy at Work

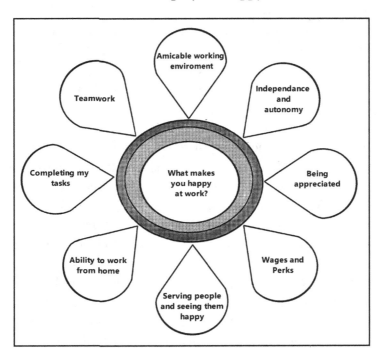

GORDEN SIMANGO, (DTL)

Job satisfaction is a positive emotional state that results from the appraisal of one's job. It is a multidimensional construct that includes satisfaction with the work itself, the pay, the benefits, the supervision, the co-workers, and the organization.

From the interviews I held with respondents for my research below are some ideas for employers to appreciate the excellence and strengths of their employees:

- **Recognize and reward employees for their accomplishments.** This can be done through formal means, such as bonuses and promotions, or through informal means, such as public recognition or simply saying thank you.
- **Provide employees with opportunities to learn and grow.** This can be done through training programs, development opportunities, or simply by giving employees challenging assignments.
- **Create a culture of appreciation.** This means making it clear that employees are valued and that their contributions are appreciated.
- **Be a good role model.** Employees are more likely to appreciate their work if they see their managers and leaders doing the same.

In my research, it was interesting to see the different ways that employees and employers perceive what makes them happy at work. For some, it is the feeling of being part of something bigger than themselves, by contributing to a greater common good. For others, it is the satisfaction of a job well done, of knowing that they are making a difference in the lives of others. For others, it is the simple pleasure of being around people they enjoy and doing work with that they find meaningful. There is no one-size fit all. What matters most is that employees feel valued and appreciated, that they have a sense of purpose in their work, and that they are able to contribute to a positive work environment. When these attributes are allowed to embed employees are more likely to be happy and productive.

Some respondents stated that their happiness in the job stems from the fact that they are continuing God's work and establishing people in God's work through their work. They believe that their work is not just a job, but a calling from God. This is a powerful motivator. For some people, work is simply a way to make a living. They may not find their work particularly meaningful, but they are content to do it as long as it provides them with the means to support themselves and their families. Others may find their work to be challenging and demanding, but they may also find it to be stimulating and rewarding.

Ultimately, what matters most is that people must find a way to make their work meaningful to them. Addisu is happy with the responsibility he has in his organization and "certainly the Lord God has given me and presided me over the church-based organization. I experience God's mercy and grace in this position, and when I sense in my spirit the Lord God saying you can do it, that makes me happy" (H. Addisu, personal communication, November 14, 2022). Kasahun is happy fulfilling his calling from God through the work he does. "I sense it is a calling. When I am serving needy people, I am also serving God. I am happy serving the needy, especially children" (T. Kasahun, personal communication, December 05, 2022).

A good supervisor propels and accelerates human flourishing. S/he leads with integrity, teaches, coaches, encourages, listens, has empathy, and models the way. Employees are content when there is cooperation among coworkers, harmony, and a sense of community at work, and when employers and employees talk openly about their struggles and triumphs and lend a hand when necessary. In this vein Kudzai shared,

> I am a vision-driven person. Apart from pursuing, knowing that every action and step that I am taking is towards the vision, I find that the satisfaction is complete when I am with the people whom I am pursuing the vision with. Not so, because they have the skills and the know-how that contribute to us achieving the mission, or whatever the objective; but it is wanting to be with them because I feel that I am valued and honored as a person within that community and that I can trust these people with my life. That makes it easier for me to wake up and go to work because together, we are happy pursuing a common vision. (M. Kudzai, personal communication, November 29, 2022)

In the same vein Kokebe is happy with most of the field workers in his organization, the majority of whom endure poor working conditions in remote areas with substandard amenities; regardless they remain steadfast and dedicated. "Their motivation drives me. I am also motivated by the potential in my organization to help the poor, the marginalized and disadvantaged; working for and with these people makes me happy" (F. Kokebe, personal communication, December 05, 2022).

A gift that workplaces can give to employees at work is having authentic relationships. Authentic relationships are those where people are open about their achievements, their struggles, and their pains, and they can relate in ways that create a sense of oneness and belonging. Isayas said in workplaces that seek to flourish human talent "people are open to celebrating successes, feeling vulnerable and still feeling accepted in their moments of brokenness, and having a space to be who they truly are, that makes me happy" (A. Isayas, personal communication, November 29, 2022).

Nothing could be more satisfying than seeing the results of one's labor. A phrase for this satisfaction is having a - direct line of sight - to one's customers or target audience and the outcomes of the work one does. That satisfaction undoubtedly gives employees joy, which may radiate to the workplace. Nahome mentioned that "the improvement I witness in people's lives after helping them makes me the happiest. I envision them being self-sufficient and faring better than they were before the assistance" (S. Nahome, personal communication, November 29, 2022). On the other hand, opportunities for development, the potential for advancement, and access to employers, make employees happy.

Those in leadership positions, part of their satisfaction rises from seeing employees happy. Negash said,

> If staff feel happy, the organization is productive, and this increases the capacity of the organization to achieve its mission and helps in itself to create a conducive environment where the organization delivers on its mission and strategic goals. (B. Negash, personal communication, November 29, 2022)

In concurrence, Kasahun said he is happy when organizations balance the achievement of the organizational goals and cares for employees at the same time. He said,

> Staff working in non-conducive environments striving to achieve better results must be acknowledged and appreciated. Never at any given point must employers entertain the thinking that they are doing employees a favor by having them on their payroll at a time when many roam the streets jobless. It is only acceptable, fair, and just that employers understand the needs of employees, perceptions, expectations, thinking, and feelings (T. Kasahun, personal communication, December 05, 2022).

Fekadu is happy when he sees and or experiences the fruits of his labour. He says,

> when I was successful in running the enterprise, and it was profitable; that gave me joy; though there was less material benefit. I did not get as much money, but I was happy that God had blessed my work. I am happy that God used me to bring blessing to the nation, and to His church. (N. Fekadu, personal communication, December 05, 2022)

SOME KEY TAKEAWAYS

Workers spend a significant part of their lifetime at work; hence workplaces must be spaces where they find joy or actively pursue it.

Opportunity to serve the needy:

Most not-for-profits provide an opportunity for workers to serve the needy. For some serving the need is in response to their faith, which strongly encourages them to serve others and the underprivileged. This can be a fulfilling experience. Most not-for-profits have a mission to improve society, and to help people in difficult situations. This enables employees to directly contribute toward a cause they believe in and to make a positive impact on the world around them. For individuals whose faith or belief systems value altruism, this aspect of serving the needy can be especially significant to them, for it may provide them an opportunity to channel their energy into something meaningful that aligns with their personal beliefs.

Cooperation and harmony in the workplace:

Successful workplaces are those that foster a sense of camaraderie, cooperation, and interpersonal harmony. Workers do better in workplaces where there is a genuine sense of community between management and staff. Cooperation and harmony in the workplace are essential for a successful business. There are many ways to foster cooperation and harmony in the workplace. One way is to create a culture of constructive workplace dissent. This will help to build trust and respect, which is essential for success. Another way to promote cooperation is to provide employees with opportunities to collaborate on projects. This will help them to learn from each other and develop new skills. Additionally, it will give them a sense of ownership over the work they are doing.

Below are some ideas for fostering cooperation and harmony in the workplace:

- **Set clear expectations.** Make sure that everyone on the team knows what is expected of them. This will help to avoid confusion and conflict.
- **Be respectful of others.** Everyone deserves to be treated with respect, regardless of their position in the organization.
- **Be open to feedback.** Be willing to listen to feedback from others and use it to improve your own work.
- **Be willing to help others.** If someone is struggling, offer to help them out. This will show that you are a team player and that you care about the success of the team.
- **Celebrate successes.** When the team achieves a goal, take the time to celebrate. This will help to boost morale and create a positive work environment.

Achievement of positive results:

Seeing positive results that affect and transform the lives of beneficiaries and those they are serving gives workers a sense of satisfaction, accomplishment and joy. Whatever the results, it is important for workers to see the impact of their work. For example, they may see a decrease in crime rates after a successful anti-crime campaign, or they may see an increase in the number of students graduating from high school after a successful education program. This can increase the employees' sense of purpose and meaning in life.

Opportunities for growth:

Opportunities for growth are essential for employee satisfaction and retention. When employees feel like they are learning and growing in their jobs, they are more likely to be engaged. Additionally, opportunities for growth can help employees to develop new skills and knowledge, which can make them more useful to the organization.

One other way to provide opportunities for growth is to offer job enrichment opportunities. Job enrichment opportunities can help employees to feel more challenged and engaged in their work. They can also help employees to develop new skills and knowledge.

Providing opportunities for growth is a win-win for both employees and organizations. Employees who feel that they are learning and growing in their jobs are more likely to be satisfied and productive.

The love of God takes precedence:

With the love of God, leaders can model the way and make employees their own business. Workplaces that demonstrate love and compassion attract talented people too. When employees are motivated by love, they are more likely to be kind, generous, and helpful. They are also more likely to be patient, tolerant, and forgiving. When employees feel loved and respected, they are more likely to be engaged in their work.

Reward constructive dissent behavior:

When employers see, acknowledge, and reward good behavior, the employees will know what is acceptable and what is not. Goodwill dissent if celebrated will encourage others to follow suit. It is important to reward constructive dissent because it gives information that helps to improve decision-making and problem-solving. When employees feel comfortable sharing their dissenting opinions, this generates more thinking that is critical, and can bring in innovative solutions or breakthrough ideas.

Communicate and share information:

Important information must never be the privy of a few in an organization. Critical information that allows employees to function well must be shared with all. It is not enough for employers to be able to communicate and instruct; they must also possess or develop the ability to listen. When employees are kept informed of important decisions and changes, they are more likely to be engaged. Additionally, open communication can help to build trust and respect between employees and employers.

Certainty:

A workplace needs certainty and predictability. When employees are not able to predict the likely responses and outcomes of their constructive dissent, they are likely to shut themselves out. Relations must be valued and built with both fairness and positive corrective behavior, and not always negative reprimands. When employees know what to expect, they are more likely to be engaged. Additionally, certainty and predictability can help to reduce stress and anxiety in the workplace.

Informal interactions:

Employers ought to create spaces and time for informal interactions among staff; organizations must also find ways to have informal interactions feeding into the formal spaces of organizations.

It is important for employers to find ways to have informal interactions feeding into the formal spaces of organizations. This can be done by encouraging employees to share ideas and feedback during informal interactions. Additionally, employers can use informal interactions to get to know their employees better and to understand their needs and concerns.

Vulnerabilities:

Workplaces with psychological safety allow for employees to feel comfortable being vulnerable in the assurance and faith that their coworkers will be available to help them recover and grow. Psychological safety is a shared belief that a team is safe for interpersonal risk taking. It allows employees to take risks and share their ideas. When employees feel safe taking risks, they are more likely to be creative.

Autonomy, and decision making:

Autonomy is the ability to make decisions and act independently. Employees must be allowed to make decisions in their portfolios. Decisions must be made as close as possible to where they have to be implemented, not by leadership only but by staff as well. Employees are more satisfied with their jobs when they are given a degree of autonomy and are encouraged to use their own initiative in completing tasks and coming up with viable solutions.

Chapter 7

LEADERSHIP PERSPECTIVES ON GOODWILL DISSENT, EMOTIONAL WELLBEING & HUMAN FLOURISHING

Calling Based Leadership

According to Hirschi et al. (2018), living out one's calling is emerging as a key construct in understanding subjective achievements at work, including general well-being; and it has greater correlations with life satisfaction, career dedication, work meaning, and job satisfaction. It is humanity's call to manifest its distinctive Christlikeness. Reju (2022) explained that in calling-based leadership, the leader attempts to understand God-given gifts, experiences, and opportunities in understanding their unique role as a called instrument of Christ's changing work in and above world cultures (slides 43, 55). Hamilton said

> We refer to it as a 'call' because it calls to us, from a future. If the call gets our attention, our concern, we pursue that call. Like we see a vision of what is possible, or we hear a voice calling out, and we follow it, and work towards making it a reality. (Hamilton, personal communication, July 18, 2022)

One's calling can be formed by a deep conviction drawn from the depths of one's soul in response to what God is revealing to do in His ministry (Bakke Graduate University, 2016). A calling for bringing happiness to the workplace and finding well-intended meaning in the voices of others to improve workplaces for the glory of God is an example.

Regardless of whether one is misunderstood or what others may think, one ought to remain committed to their calling. Responding to a call can be costly, requiring significant sacrifice in the face of adversity, and even opposition from within one's inner self. Calling is critical because it provides people with a perspective of purpose, direction, and resilience in their pursuit of what God has purposed and predestined them for.

However, finding one's true calling can be scary. Out of the many conflicting choices, there is a voice within all the choices, and one needs to pray for a spirit of discernment and where God is leading them to, because in most cases they cannot see themselves going there. Examples in the Bible can be drawn from Moses (Who, and why me?), Gideon (Why me?), Jonah (Not me!), Isaiah (Send me!), and from the Acts of the Apostles (Exodus 3:11 – 18, Judges 6, Jonah 1, Acts 9).

God is the beginning and the end; without Him, nothing exists. According to Guinness (1998), God first calls people to Himself, meaning people are not first called to a special task. Being devoted to no one or anything more than God to whom people are called and for Him is the key to answering and obeying the call (p. 43). "Responding to the call means rising to the challenge, but in conversation and in partnership – and in an intimate relationship between the called and the caller" (Guinness, 1998, p. 24).

Calling-based leadership is a leadership style that is based on the belief that leaders are called to their position by a higher power. Calling-based leaders believe that they are not in charge of their own destiny, but that they are following a path that has been set out for them by God or another higher power.

Calling-based leaders are often motivated by a sense of purpose and mission. They believe that they are called to make a difference in the world, and they are willing to sacrifice their own personal needs and desires in order to fulfill their calling.

Calling-based leadership can be a very effective leadership style. However, it is important to note that calling-based leaders are not always successful. In some cases, calling-based leaders may be led astray by their own ego or by their own selfish interpretation of what their calling is.

INCARNATIONAL LEADERSHIP

Incarnational leaders can enter into the world of those whose challenges they seek to share and understand, an exemplary leader of incarnational leadership being the Lord and Savior Jesus Christ (John 1:4). In this pursuit, ethnographers spend a lot of time with the group being studied (Creswell & Creswell, 2017).

The Lord and Savior Jesus Christ mixed with people, including outcasts, and wished for their good. He exhibited compassion and kindness to them, was honest in his interactions with them, and won their hearts.

Leaders ought to be sincerely interested in their employees' well-being to bring human flourishing. "And the Word (Christ) became flesh, and lived among us; and we [actually] saw His glory, glory as belongs to the [One and] only begotten *Son* of the Father, [the Son who is truly unique, the only One of His kind, who is] full of grace and truth (absolutely free of deception)" (John 1:14). Truth and grace are attributes of transformational leadership.

Leaders operating the values of grace and truth empathize. They work from a perspective of the realities of the contexts in which they are leading. Leaders cannot create a happy working environment by watching from the terraces, but by immersing themselves in the spaces where people are at work (Colon, 2012). Hamilton (personal communication, July 18, 2022) shared the following insights.

> In the US, there is a TV show called Undercover Boss. The CEO goes undercover or incarnates as a new employee at the workplace where employees won't recognize them. They learn about how things are going for the employees who are doing the workday in and day out, and then they reward and promote those employees who show loyalty and integrity. The CEO also learns how to lead better based on what they discover.

Certainly, not all leaders can be undercover bosses, but truly they can create time to spend with workers on the work floor, working with and listening to their employees, contrary to them building walls around themselves, and getting the non-budging personal assistant who seal all roads leading to 'the boss'; and certainly sitting in an affluent office adorned with wall hangings and artworks engrained with the organizational values of Love, Care, Employee engagement, Listening etc. Aren't these just mere words on the walls?

CONTEXTUAL LEADERSHIP

Contextual leadership calls for relevance in the environment of a leader (Cultural Atlas, n.d.). Adaptability could be one of its related concepts. Leaders ought to change their style and approach to fit the culture, context, or condition of an organization (Cultural Atlas, n.d.). The Cultural Atlas (n.d.) further opined that in the twenty-first century, leaders should pay attention to the context, while also understanding that contexts are not static. Leaders don't just change culture; culture is changing, and leaders may seek to influence it, guide it, or flow with it.

Trompenaars and Hampden-Turner (1997) gave the following example.

> What matters is not what they are or where [a global food outlet or a music gadget] are physically found, but what they mean to the people in each society. The essence of culture is not what is visible on the surface. It refers to how members in a group comprehend and interpret the world. So, while the fact that we can all listen to Walkmans and eat hamburgers indicates that there are certain unique items that may be offered with a universal message, it does not indicate what eating hamburgers or listening to Walkmans means in different cultures. (p. 3)

Even though leadership and management principles may be universal, the way in which happiness in the workplace and constructive workplace dissent manifest varies depending on the setting. This is why contextualization is necessary. Contextual leaders can adapt their leadership style to the needs of the situation. They are also able to build relationships with their followers and create a positive work environment.

SHALOM LEADERSHIP

Franklin (2020) wrote,

> The use of *shalom* in the Old Testament is wide-ranging because it refers to wholeness, well-being, abundant life, satisfactory conditions, completeness, soundness, peace, well-being, and salvation. It describes the way the world ought to be - the vision of an integrated whole of all manner of relationships. It implies a state of mind that is at peace and is satisfied and nothing is lacking. People and their communities are characterized in their relationships with each other, God, and creation as being just, peaceful, harmonious, and enjoyable. It envisions

a new community that breaks down the barriers of language, economy, race, gender, and nationalism. (p. 10)

From this definition, shalom is the integrated totality of connections, in the workplace, healthful human ties, and a contended state of mind, emotional wellbeing and human flourishing (Franklin, 2020). I also propose a shalom leadership in a working environment which is free of rigidity in hierarchy, silos, hatred, ethnicity, among others. In shalom leadership, employees are considered as coworkers, cooperating together; and goodwill dissent is seen as contributing to God's purpose for work, which is to glorify Him. A leadership style that cultivates shalom recognizes the presence of the living God in others. Shalom leadership can be practiced in a number of ways, including carefully listening to the other person's point of view and giving feedback in a manner that edifies their talents.

Shalom leaders are committed to justice, equity, and compassion. They are also committed to building relationships and creating community. Shalom leaders are not afraid to stand up for what they believe in, even when it is unpopular. They are also willing to listen to others and learn from them.

Below are some ideas on Shalom leadership:

- **Justice:** Shalom leaders are committed to justice. They believe that everyone should have the opportunity to thrive and that no one should be oppressed or marginalized.
- **Equity:** Shalom leaders are committed to equity. They believe that everyone should have equal access to resources and opportunities.
- **Compassion:** Shalom leaders are compassionate. They care about the well-being of others and they are willing to help those in need.
- **Relationship building:** Shalom leaders are good at building relationships. They can connect with others on a personal level and they are able to build trust.
- **Community building:** Shalom leaders are good at building community. They can bring people together and they are able to create a sense of belonging.
- **Listening to others:** Shalom leaders are good listeners. They are able to listen to others with empathy and understanding.
- **Learning from others:** Shalom leaders are willing to learn from others. They are open to new ideas, and they are willing to change their minds when presented with new information.

SERVANT LEADERSHIP

In the servant leadership model, the leader's attitude, conduct, and priority are on serving others and are exhibited through sincere and passionate service. In servant leadership "the leader leads by serving, and serves by leading" (Reju, 2022, slide 26). Servant leadership is godly and biblical.

> But Jesus called them to Himself and said, "You know that the rulers of the Gentiles have absolute power *and* lord it over them, and their great men exercise authority over them [tyrannizing them]. It is not this way among you, but whoever wishes to become great among you shall be your servant, and whoever wishes to be first among you shall be your [willing and humble] slave; just as the Son of Man did not come to be served, but to serve, and to give His life as a ransom for many [paying the price to set them free from the penalty of sin]." (Matthew 20:25-28)

The Lord and Savior, Jesus Christ goes on to teach that in servant leadership, regardless of title or position, one ought to lower him/herself and not think highly of themselves.

Servant leadership also stems from a willingness to be humble "Therefore, whoever humbles himself like this child is greatest in the kingdom of heaven" (Matthew 18:4). Matthew 23 in the Bible depicts servant leaders who not only preach, but also live out the teachings of the Word of God. Through exercising servant leadership, leaders pay attention to employee voices, foster a positive work environment, and recognizing God's image in others (Matthew 23). The transformational angle that Christ taught is that the "the greatest among you shall be your servant" (Matthew 23:11).

Servant leaders are concerned about the welfare of their staff and seek partnership with God to restore strained workplace relationships where they exist. The utmost good of Christ should descend to people to draw the reality they desire if they are to actualize it (Guinness, 1998, p. 14).

There are many benefits to servant leadership. Servant leaders create a positive and productive work environment, their team members are more likely to be happy and engaged in their work, and they are more likely to be successful. Servant leaders are also humble and willing to learn from others. Servant leaders are often seen as role models by their team members. They are respected and trusted, and their team members are willing to go the extra mile for them.

Chapter 8

INVESTING AND RESOURCING

One way to invest and resource and make emotional wellbeing, goodwill dissent, and human flourishing a reality is to introduce staff welfare programs that promote workplace safety and prevent all forms of harassment; whilst ensuring freedom of expression within established standard operating procedures (SOPs). In ensuring safe workspaces, key informants suggested that employers must ensure that computers, furniture and lighting are safe for human health. Organizations must also consider team building activities, and where possible sporting events, as part of a staff wellness program.

Further in thinking of staff welfare, Yidnekachew shared that,

> Employers might do well by thinking of personal fellowship times for workers, to spend time together. For example, in my organization, once a year we have a trip of one week together to unwind, decompress and to refresh our minds out of the usual working environment. This demonstrates that my organization does not only want employees' attention to work but is also concerned about their welfare. Organizations may also consider giving staff training and refresher courses out of organizational time. (A. Yidnekachew, personal communication, December 5, 2022)

To gain knowledge, some interviewees suggested that one must be willing to learn, by inviting someone with excellence in the issues or the subject at hand to witness to them, in service to God.

Sometimes organizational structures impede joy at work, emotional wellbeing, and goodwill dissent. Amanueal said, "Human potential, emotional wellbeing, goodwill dissent will not flourish under organizational systems that do not foster optimal growth of employees.

Employers must also not only think of giving employees duties, but also consider employee rights (Amanueal, personal communication, November 30, 2022).

Kudzai shared that,

> I believe it is best for organizations to take away routine? We have manuals where we have written that we must do things in this way. Why not give people a picture of the end goal of the desired outcome? Say this is where we want to end up; this is what we want to achieve. How are you going to do it and get there; then allow people to apply their talents, and their skills, and to engage their minds, to connect and to work together on an idea. I think that helps workers to have a level of responsibility, ownership, and creativity. In summary I would say throw the end goal, and say chat the path, and allow people to do it their own way. (M. Kudzai, personal communication, November 30, 2022)

Organizational commitments may do well in situations where they are supported by policy. Doing so brings in organizational commitment. "With policy there is a high probability that the commitments will be addressed or improved" Biruk, personal communication, December 6, 2022).

Employees must develop new skills or expand on existing ones. Employees need to invest in developing professionally and personally. Organizations may also do well in providing training, mentoring and demonstrating exemplary leadership.

> In teaching and mentoring, to avoid making the individual receiving guidance feel like they are a student, leaders must avoid acting as though they are teaching, and the other person is learning. Leaders must speak in humble ways to avoid negatively impacting the mind of the other. (B. Negash, personal communication, November 29, 2022)

Learning from God About Oneself?

Employers and Employees must learn from God to respect others and to recognize the image of God in the other. God Himself is in charge of every situation. Jesus tells His followers that they are His friends. "You are my friends if you do what I command you" (John 15:14); Christ is the bread of life "I am the bread of life; whoever comes to me shall not hunger, and whoever believes in me shall never thirst" (John 6:35). People are called to care for one another, both as employers and as employees. "I am the good shepherd. The good shepherd lays down his life for the sheep" (John 10:11). Haregewoin said,

> When my mind is disturbed, I cannot hear God. I cannot hear Him when I am angry, but I can see Him in the eyes of needy people, literally meaning only when I have emotional wellbeing am I able to see God. When I am agitated, I honestly find it hard to see God. (D. Haregowoin, personal communication, December 6, 2022)

Micromanaging and too much control brings frustrations at work. Hanan said,

> God is currently teaching me about control. Not only are you releasing others when you surrender control; you are also releasing yourself. Within the community of God also then the Holy Spirit moves and begins to complete all those pieces that relate to identity, purpose, and destiny and responding to questions such as who am I am really, what am I on earth to achieve, and what has God given me in the toolbox as tools to achieve. (Hanan, personal communication, November 30, 2022)

God is all-powerful. As His children humanity must worship Him ceaselessly; in all facets of their lives; be even through their jobs. In this case it is important to take work as worship. When stapling those papers at work, staple them like you are stapling for God, sweep like you are sweeping for God, analyze like you are analyzing for God. Always strive for perfection. Workplaces allow employees to put words and aspirations into action. "Our place of employment serves as the pulpit, or platform where we live out our Christian faith to the glory of God" (A. Netsanet, personal communication, November 29, 2022). In concurrence, Dr. Zachary would say, "99% of Christians will never give a sermon from the stage or pulpit [depending on the practice and doctrine of their religion]. However, our lives can be a sermon, and our platform for influence, such as our daily work, is our pulpit" (Z. Hamilton, personal communication, April 24, 2022).

Furthermore, interviewees shared that one is not going to be on a job forever. An employee runs their race and must be prepared to give the baton to the next person when the time comes. When the time comes, leaders need to be prepared to give the baton to the next person. This means that leaders need to train and develop their employees. Leaders need to share their knowledge and experience with employees. They also need to be supportive and encouraging as employees take on new responsibilities.

It is also important to remember that leaders are not the only ones who are running a race. Their colleagues are also running their own races. Leaders need to be supportive of them and help them to succeed. When leaders work together with employees and support them, they can create a positive and productive work environment. Leaders can also help each other to achieve set goals and to reach their full potential.

Below are some ideas for preparing to give the baton to the next person:

- **Start early.** Do not wait until you are ready to retire to start thinking about succession planning. Start early and give yourself plenty of time to train and develop others.
- **Be clear about your expectations.** Make sure that your mentee knows what is expected of them. This includes their responsibilities, their goals, and their deadlines.
- **Provide support.** Be available to answer questions and provide support to your mentee. This will help them to succeed in their roles.
- **Be patient.** It takes time for someone to learn a new job. Be patient with your mentees and give them the time they need to succeed.
- **Celebrate successes.** When your mentee achieves a goal, celebrate their success. This will show them that you are supportive of them and that you are proud of their accomplishments.

When leaders are prepared to give the baton to the next person, they can create a smooth and successful transition.

Clarissa says:

> In realizing that jobs are not permanent places everlasting, God is teaching me that leaders are able to raise other people who will take over from them. The final form of leadership is legacy. Leaders come and go; they are not eternal. A leader's job should be to train, equip, and prepare those who will take over their positions. (F. Clarissa personal communication, November 29, 2022)

Employees and employers must feel valuable before God, and that they are accountable to Him in life and for the leadership roles entrusted to them. Employees and employers must be responsible in their jobs and lead exemplary lives. This means that employees and employers must live their lives in a way that honors God and brings glory to His name. They must also be responsible in their jobs and use their talents and abilities to serve others. This means that they must be honest, hardworking, and reliable. They must also be respectful of their colleagues and customers.

God also instructs employers and employees to emulate the way that the Lord Jesus Christ conducted Himself and set the standard for human behavior. The Lord Jesus Christ was the perfect example of how to live a life that is pleasing to God. He was humble, kind, and compassionate. He always put others before Himself. Leaders should strive to follow His example in their own lives.

Negash shared,

> Because of Him [God], I feel valuable in the eyes of others. Additionally, I am aware of my obligation to Him [God] to live my life in accordance with His

principles and to point others to Him. I have a responsibility to lead myself, my work, and others around me, whether they are connected to God or not. In terms of how I relate to the people in my immediate environment, I should set an example for them by loving, respecting, and giving them value. I should also serve them. (B. Negash, personal communication, November 29, 2022)

Sharing along the same vein, Tsegahun said,

I consider that good stewardship is crucial. As the head of the organization, I am a custodian. I oversee partnerships, programs, finances, staff relationships, and many other areas. We are all individuals with various organizational roles, and duties, besides our levels in the organizational hierarchy; we are all vital components of the organization. I must thus treat others with care and dignity. I must show them respect. I must acknowledge employees and serve them with a servant leadership mindset. (G. Tsegahun, personal communication, November 14, 2022)

What God is Teaching About Himself

God is teaching and revealing that He is everlasting. Employees and employers must continue to learn from God. God created humanity for His own purpose, and in His own image

God is the creator of the universe and everything in it. He is eternal and everlasting, and He has been teaching and revealing Himself to humanity since the beginning of time. God created humanity for His own purpose. This means that humanity is created to be like Him, to love Him, and to serve Him. Humanity is also created to have dominion over the earth and to care for it. God continues to teach and reveal Himself to people today. He does this through His Word, the Bible, through His creation, and through His Spirit. Humanity can learn about God by studying His Word, by observing His creation, discernment and by praying and seeking Him. Genet said I need this assurance "because sometimes when I realize my weaknesses I get frustrated" (B. Genet, personal communication, November 29, 2022). God is teaching employers and employees to be exemplary to others, loving, valuing, and respecting. God is teaching employers and employees compassion, kindness, and the fruits of the Holy Spirit. God is teaching about stewarding others in fulfilling ways. "For I was hungry, and you gave me food, I was thirsty, and you gave me drink, I was a stranger and you welcomed me" (Matthew 25:35). Nebyou said,

I feel I am my brother's keeper. I feel a yearning in my spirit to help our employees more when I visit them in the field and witness the work they are doing. Serving people, in my opinion, is more valuable than anything else. We have a wonderful opportunity to serve God's people and God Himself thorough our work, and the people we meet in this mission. We must not only do it for a salary. (T. Nebyou, personal communication, December 05, 2022)

In working with people, both the employers and the employees must feel a great sense of stewardship. It is therefore important that both employers and employees realize that each person is of their own kind and is a gift from God. What employers and employees may do best is to edify co-workers as opposed to fighting them. It is a duty. In working with people, both the employers and the employees must feel a great sense of stewardship. This means that they must take responsibility for the well-being of their co-workers and for the success of the organization. It also means that employees must be willing to put the needs of the organization above their own.

When employers and employees work together in a spirit of stewardship, they can create a workplace that is both productive and enjoyable. They can also build relationships that are based on respect, trust, and cooperation. This can lead to more successful organizations and more fulfilling work experience for everyone involved.

Here, Immanuel said,

> According to what I am learning about God, God does not place people in positions of authority by chance. He has a plan for everything He does. In my leadership role I try to find the plan of God which I must accomplish for His Glory. For what God is teaching me about others, I always take it from a point of view that there is a God given potential in the other. My role therefore is to cultivate that potential God has put in the other person. (S. Immanuel, personal communication, November 29, 2022)

The love for God, and the love for humanity must not be confined to a specific place, like at work but also in homes, including to those who are not of the same bloodline. Ropa said,

> We need to value people, not only in organizations, but also in our homes. We have housemaids. Sometimes we ignore their contribution. We focus on their failures, sometimes minimum and minor faults. Human beings are created in the image of God. Even those in the lowest status of society, they have value. It is only by God's grace that we are in a privileged position; but on humanity level we are equal. (S. Ropa, personal communication, November 29, 2022)

Organizational commitment

Several policy documents in organizations gather dust on the shelves. It is sometimes hard to trace those policy pronouncements in the lifeblood of organizations. Oftentimes policy can be reduced to be mere on paper with little practice

Below are some ideas for ensuring that policies are followed:

- Ensure that the policies are current and relevant to the organization's needs.
- Ensure that the policies are feasible and attainable.
- Ensure that the policies are adaptable enough to changes in the organization's environment.
- Ensure that policies are effectively communicated to staff.
- Ensure that policies are consistently and uniformly enforced.
- Ensure that policies are reviewed on a regular basis and changed as needed.

In this vein of the discussion, Diriba said,

> With regard to policy, I believe that because of how it has been applied in the contemporary workplace, we quickly associate policy with being restrictive. If policy is about how to play the game so that everyone is free to express themselves and explore their skills, then policy is about how to encourage everyone to speak up and contribute. This way policy becomes a vehicle to eliminate barriers to people's freedom of expression. If we affirm that we cherish employees, then the substance of our policies should reflect this principle. (Z. Diriba, personal communication, December 05, 2022)

Employers may implement strategies like rewarding and recognizing employees. Employees should be rewarded for doing the right thing, especially if they are expressing goodwill dissent by doing their jobs in inventive ways to benefit the organization, their coworkers, and even external stakeholders. Respondents agreed that certain executives and employees have a natural tendency to believe that dissent always has consequences that are detrimental. This may be informed by their experience.

Respondents mentioned that employers may do well by creating rules and a culture that moots respect for each other and respect for the systems of the organization. "When you do this people do not wait for your command, or presence, but the system itself will work to the advantage of both the organization and the employees" (C. Zerihun, personal communication, December 05, 2022).

Policy can also be about how leaders manage and supervise; a former BGU graduate student said,

In my reaction to this, I find myself drawn to Denis Bakke. He was an excellent industrialist, and corporate executive. He added value to others. He hired qualified people to build his business, and he gave them the freedom to decide, but also to consult one another. As a result, they developed problem-solving skills. People were pleased to learn that they could make decisions and were given the authority to do so. If there was anything beyond their scope, they would refer it to the higher level. If leaders want continuity in their legacy, they should not only work on the production of materials they are working with, but they must also develop people to take over their responsibilities. (J. Selamawit, personal communication, October 27, 2022)

Recommended next steps

Employers must embrace goodwill dissent. It builds up organizations and must never be seen as negative. Goodwill dissent can be a valuable tool for organizations, as it can help to identify problems, generate new ideas, and improve decision-making. It can help to identify problems that may not be apparent to management. Employees who are close to the work may have insights that management does not have.

Misgana recommended employers to increase capacities of employees.

Increasing employee capacity is crucial, in my experience. A high staff capacity will naturally result in fewer conflicts. One's perfection levels rise as his/her ability does. This then may lead to workers experiencing higher degrees of job satisfaction, emotional wellbeing, and goodwill dissent. Lack of confidence prevents employees from feeling psychologically safe, therefore it is important for organizations to teach employees confidence-building skills but also for employees to self-develop. (J. Misgana, personal communication, October 27, 2022)

Rather than relying solely on internal metrics to determine success, organizations should start asking for feedback from a wider range of stakeholders, such as members of the local community, service providers, customers, and government agencies, among other external stakeholders. External stakeholders can provide a different perspective on the organization's performance. They may see things that the organization's employees or management do not see. External stakeholders can provide valuable feedback on the organization's services, and on the organization's impact on the community; and may identify ways in which the organization can be more socially responsible. Seeking feedback from external stakeholders is an important part of being a responsible organization. The organization should also communicate its plans to the stakeholders and keep them updated on its progress.

Here Tendai said,

> An organization may consider hearing from stakeholders who are receiving assistance from staff of the organization. When we sit together, we can always believe that we are angels and that everything we do is right. However, if we rise above ourselves and allow others to evaluate us, we might be amazed at what God may reveal to us. (M. Tendai, personal communication, November 29, 2022)

SOME KEY TAKEAWAYS

Emotional wellbeing and Goodwill dissent are important for nurturing employee talents. In this sense, a number of crucial pillars are necessary to support this, including the following:

Staff welfare:

the requirement for staff welfare programs with the goals of enhancing workplace safety, preventing harassment, and guaranteeing freedom of expression within the confines of predetermined standard operating procedures (SOPs), so as to prevent the instigation of disruptive behaviours within the workplace is important. It is also possible for employers to meet the spiritual requirements of their workforce, for example by providing spaces within the workplace where staff members are free to worship. Staff retreats, with a balance of productive work, stimulating activities, and relaxing downtime, must be considered too.

There are many different ways to improve staff welfare. One is to provide a safe and healthy work environment. This includes things like providing adequate ventilation, lighting, and noise control. Another is to offer flexible work arrangements. This can include things like telecommuting, flextime, and compressed workweeks. Employers can also provide employees with confidential counseling and support. Promoting teamwork, providing recognition, and celebrating successes can also improve staff welfare.

Valuing Employee Talents:

Employers and coworkers alike should make an effort to recognize and value the abilities of their fellow employees. In a broad sense, having a grateful attitude is equivalent to recognizing the talents of other people. Furthermore, organizations need to acknowledge the value of their highest-performing employees and invest in their careers in ways that are beneficial to the organization. Valuing employee talents is essential for any organization that wants to succeed. When employees feel valued, they are more likely to be engaged in their work and feel like they are making a difference. This can lead to increased productivity, improved morale, and reduced turnover.

Training and raising consciousness:

Employers must consider providing employees with orientation, ongoing training, and periodic refresher courses, as well as certification opportunities. Employees should be willing to learn new things and to develop their abilities. The more capacity staff have, the more chances that an organization will achieve its end goals. Staff with high capacity also have more confidence to voice their concerns with goodwill dissent.

There are many different ways to provide training and development opportunities for employees. Some of the most common methods include:

- **On-the-job training:** This is the most common type of training, and it involves providing employees with the opportunity to learn new skills while they are working.
- **Classroom training:** This type of training involves providing employees with formal instruction in a classroom setting.
- **Online training:** This type of training is becoming increasingly popular, and it involves providing employees with access to online courses and resources.
- **Mentoring:** This type of training involves pairing employees with more experienced employees who can provide them with guidance and support.
- **Coaching:** This type of training involves working with employees one-on-one to help them develop their skills and abilities.

In addition to providing training and development opportunities, organizations should also create a culture of learning and growth. This means encouraging employees to take risks, try new things, and share their knowledge and experience with others.

Guide, coach and mentor:

Coaching is an asking model pulling out of people through questions their own experience, education, and expertise. Mentoring is a telling model of pouring into people one's experience, education and expertise. All learning must be mutual. If employees feel that the mentorship provided by leaders is an attempt to put them down, then learning will fail.

Below are some ideas for managers who want to create a positive and supportive work environment where employees feel comfortable learning and growing:

- **Focus on coaching.** When employees make mistakes, do not just tell them what they did wrong. Instead, ask them questions that will help them to understand the mistake and how to avoid making it in the future.
- **Focus on mentoring.** Employees are always eager to learn from their more experienced colleagues. Be willing to share your knowledge and experience with them and help them to develop their own skills and talents.
- **Create a culture of learning.** Encourage employees to take risks and try new things. Let them know that it's okay to make mistakes, but they must also learn from them.

- **Be a role model.** Employees are more likely to learn and grow if they see their managers doing the same. Managers must be role models for their supervisees by constantly learning and growing themselves.

Build flatter organization:

Under inept systems of hierarchical organization, human potential in the form of emotional wellness, goodwill dissent, and human flourishing would not thrive. Organizational structures must promote and support a conducive working environment. In creating organizational hierarchies' organizations must not only be structured to give employees duties, but also to think of their rights.

A flat organization is one with fewer levels of hierarchy. This can lead to a number of benefits, including increased employee satisfaction, improved communication, and greater innovation. When employees have more autonomy and decision-making power, they are more likely to be engaged in their work. When there are fewer levels of hierarchy, it is easier for employees to communicate with each other and with management. This can lead to faster decision-making and a more efficient workflow.

However, there are also some challenges associated with flat organizations. One challenge is that it can be difficult to manage a large organization without a clear hierarchy. It is important to have clear lines of communication and to make sure that everyone knows who is responsible for what.

Overall, flat organizations can offer a number of benefits. However, it is important to be aware of the challenges associated with them before implementing an absolute flat structure. Standardized policies help to ensure that decisions are consistent and can be reliably anticipated. Policies are a representation of an organization's commitment, but they are also a demonstration of the organization's willingness to be held accountable for their implementation, or lack thereof. Rather than focusing solely on imposing limits, policies must provide guidance on how to foster positive work environments that encourage healthy debate and mutual respect.

What God is telling about self, Himself, and others:

In designing successful work interventions employers and employees must discern what God is saying and how an organization's plan aligns with His will or preferable future. It is essential to keep in mind that humankind is God's agent to advance His will on earth as it is in heaven, and that every human creation must consider God in their stewardship of others, as well as themselves.

In order to design successful work interventions and create an environment that aligns with God's will, it is important to understand what God is saying about self, Himself, and others. Employers and employees must be stewards of each other. As such, it is important to create a workplace culture that values and respects every person and treats them with kindness, compassion, and fairness. Employers and employees have a responsibility to steward resources well. This means that in the workplace, employers and employees should strive to use their time, talents, and resources in a way that is responsible and ethical.

Apply emotional wellbeing, goodwill dissent and joy at work as Siamese twins:
The three concepts work well together, and the accomplishment of one lead to the accomplishment of the other two. When employees feel emotionally well, they are more likely to be open to dissenting opinions. By applying emotional wellbeing, goodwill dissent, and joy at work as Siamese twins, organizations can leverage the synergies between these concepts to create a strong and sustainable workplace culture.

Creating a robust feedback mechanism:
Robust feedback mechanisms are crucial for businesses and organizations that want to continuously improve their operations and ensure that their employees, stakeholders, customers, and partners are satisfied with the services they provide. By allowing staff and external stakeholders to provide feedback, employers can identify areas where they need to improve, and take action to address issues that may arise.

Proactiveness in identifying future challenges and opportunities:
It is important for organizations to think of a pillar that encompasses a scan of the environment in order to identify future challenges and opportunities. Looking to the present and into the future whilst presenting the organization with cutting-edge intelligence, emerging from research, innovation, and futuristic forecasting is important.

Proactiveness in identifying future challenges and opportunities is essential for organizations that want to stay ahead of the curve. By scanning the environment and identifying potential challenges and opportunities, organizations can take steps to mitigate the risks and capitalize on opportunities.

Below are some ideas for organizations that want to be more proactive in identifying future challenges and opportunities:

- **Create a culture of innovation and creativity.** Encourage employees to think outside the box and come up with new ideas.
- **Invest in research and development.** This will help you stay ahead of the curve on emerging trends and technologies.
- **Monitor the competition.** Learn what they are doing well and what they are not doing so well.
- **Talk to your customers and suppliers.** Get their insights on the market and what they are looking for.
- **Be prepared to change.** The world is constantly changing, so you need to be prepared to adapt.
- **Be flexible.** Do not be afraid to try new things and change course if necessary.
- **Be patient.** It takes time to identify and capitalize on future challenges and opportunities.

Chapter 9

PRACTICING AND SUSTAINING

What seeds may be sown today

A value system that supports goodwill dissent and human flourishing is fundamental. Without it, organizations strive in vain. Employers must invest in efficient and effective governance systems. In organizations that are governed with integrity goodwill dissent is likely to be fostered. The need to instill in future generations goodwill dissent and human flourishing cannot be underestimated. Fundamentally, for nation-building, the formal education system must be impressed to incorporate principles of goodwill dissent, and human flourishing into the school curriculum. Children must be taught to be compassionate and to care about the well-being of others. They must be taught to be responsible and to take ownership of their actions. Similar concepts must also be taught in business schools and tertiary institutions.

Spaces where employees gather in a casual and informal setting to think and reflect on work-related topics or thematic areas of concern in the workplace is an idea to consider. Therein colleagues can share extraordinary insights and breakthroughs from projects they are working on or are participating in. Such spaces may assist employers to identify talent as well as ideas for innovation and revival.

Immanuel, said,

> Leaders must aim to come from a place of realizing that goodwill dissent and human flourishing are all things that can contribute to a better work environment and productivity. It is true that a happy workforce is a productive workforce. Organizations must learn continuously and re-learn. (S. Immanuel, personal communication, October 27, 2022)

For employees who are geographically dispersed but can communicate digitally, their employers may institute the practice of virtual coffee and tea breaks. This method is effective in maintaining relationships between coworkers. Virtual coffee and tea breaks can be done through video conferencing, instant messaging, or even social media.

There are many benefits to virtual coffee and tea breaks. They can help to:

- Build relationships between employees,
- Promote collaboration and teamwork,
- Increase employee morale,
- Reduce stress and burnout,
- Improve communication and coordination.

In considering implementing virtual coffee and tea breaks at your organization, it may be important to consider some of the following ideas:

- Make sure that everyone has a chance to participate. If you have a large team, you may need to break up the staff into smaller groups.
- Encourage employees to share personal stories and updates. This will help to build relationships and create a sense of community.
- Be flexible. If employees are busy, they may not be able to attend every break. Be understanding and make sure that they know that they can catch up on the conversation later.
- Evaluate the success of the breaks. Take time to reflect on how the breaks are going. Are employees enjoying them? Are they helping to improve communication and collaboration?

Language creates and shapes culture. Organizations need to look at how communication is generated, flows, and is spoken, including nonverbal communication. In doing so, organizations should evaluate whether or not their message is being received by everyone concerned, as well as the message tone and the delivery method. The way that language is used can have a big impact on the organization's culture. For example, if an organization uses language that is inclusive and respectful, it will create a more positive and productive work environment.

Below are some ideas on using language effectively in organizations:

- **Be clear and concise:** Use simple language.
- **Be respectful:** Avoid using language that is offensive or discriminatory.
- **Be inclusive:** Use language that is welcoming and inclusive.
- **Be authentic:** Use language that is genuine and reflects your organization's values.
- **Be consistent:** Use consistent language throughout your organization.

- **Be mindful of your tone:** Your tone can convey a lot of meaning, so be careful about how you use it.
- **Be aware of your audience:** Tailor your language to your audience, considering their age, culture, and other factors.
- **Be open to feedback:** Ask for feedback on your use of language and make changes as necessary.

Zeni said,

> I believe it is important for people on the ground to hear a leader saying that I would really like to hear your hearty concerns. When this happens or if it were to happen, for leaders to show that they are really listening and for them to take action afterwards is important for workers. (S. Zeni, personal communication, October 27, 2022)

It is crucial for executives to set an example while implementing a new system. A lion on paper is just that—a lion on paper; it never actually exists.

Visions only have value if they are put into action and kept alive throughout time. A lion on paper remains a lion on paper, it is never real.

If a company mandates that its workers be efficient with their time, for instance, it is the responsibility of its leadership to serve as the policy's prototype. It is the responsibility of management to instill a sense of commitment to organizational policies among workers. It is also crucial that most systems and policies be developed using a bottom-up rather than a top-down approach. This will help when the time to activate those systems comes about.

Employers must communicate with their employees about the new systems. They need to explain why a system is being implemented and what benefits it will provide. They must also be prepared to answer questions that employees may have about the system. Employers must be patient with their employees as they adjust to the new system. Employers need to be understanding and supportive during this time.

Mehdi shared the following story on the power of emphasis and echoing the vision again and again, and the power of repetition.

> Mine is on the power of repetition. The founder of my organization came in yesterday and was giving input, and imparting wisdom on how he has walked the journey of trusting God. As a result, he remarked something about vision and the necessity for repetition. Leaders must never tire of repeating themselves. Repetition leads to greater comprehension. If someone misses it the first time, they may catch it the second, third, fourth, or the fifth time it is spoken. (P. Mehdi, personal communication, November 13, 2022)

Fekadu, shared the following story that captured well the appreciative inquiry mindset, especially the discovery part.

> In my previous job, in which I served as Enterprise and Corporate Manager in the State Farms in the Horticultural Development Corporation, I used to communicate with workers, managers, supervisors, and foremen. The way that I used to approach them was always showing and appreciating the good part of their work. There is one incident in which the Plant Protection Expert was spraying chemicals for protection against insects on the farm in the citrus orchard. When I arrived there, I saw something that needed to be corrected immediately, but I held off. I started observing them, giving value to what they were doing and what they had done. I appreciated them. It was only after that, that I went into things that needed to be corrected; and the supervisor of that operation was very happy to hear my positive comments before I commented on their failures. (A. Fekadu, personal communication, December 05, 2022)

Getting the Necessary Support

Respondents' Suggestions on What Has to Be Done to Make Their Suggestions Thrive

Making suggestions thrive

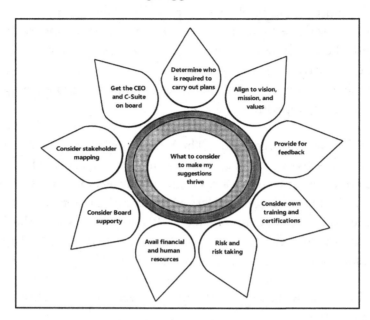

Transformation must be consistent with the vision, purpose, and values of the organization. This means that the changes that are made must be aligned with the organization's long-term goals and objectives. They must also be consistent with the organization's culture and values.

It is critical to decide who will be responsible for carrying out the plans. This means that the organization needs to identify the people who will be responsible for implementing the changes and ensure that these people have the skills and resources they need to be successful.

Stakeholder mapping is essential during planning. Stakeholder mapping assists in identifying key players and multipliers both within and outside of the organization. When promoting change, it is critical that the C-Suite supports the principles, and that the CEO is on board. This means that the organization's top leaders need to be committed to the change process. They need to be willing to provide the resources and support that is needed throughout the change process.

Leadership is essential, as is board support and dedication to strategic reforms. The leaders need to inspire and cheer lead employees during the change process. Organizations that are undergoing renewal must avoid carrying on as usual. This means that they need to be willing to make changes to the way the organization is run. They may need to change their products or services, their processes, or their culture. They need to make financial and human resources available for the regeneration process. They may need to hire new employees, train existing employees, or invest in new technologies.

Investing in building trust and holding both employers and employees accountable is important. This means that both employers and employees need to create a culture of trust and transparency. When necessary, leaders must not be hesitant to let go people who do not share the vision or work against it. This means that they need to be willing to make tough decisions.

Leaders need not shun away from taking risks, albeit understanding contextual factors to discern acceptable and non-acceptable risk. They need to be aware of the risks and to take steps to mitigate them.

When organizations are undergoing renewal, it is important to remember that change is difficult. There will be resistance to change, and there will be setbacks. However, if organizations are willing to make the necessary changes, they can emerge from renewal stronger and more successful.

Below are some ideas for organizations that are undergoing renewal:

- **Start with a clear vision.** What do you want to achieve with the renewal process? What are your goals?
- **Create a plan.** How are you going to achieve your goals? What steps do you need to take?
- **Communicate with your employees.** Keep them informed about the renewal process and get their feedback.
- **Be patient.** Change takes time. Do not expect to see results overnight.
- **Be flexible.** Things will change as you go through the renewal process. Be prepared to adapt your plans as needed.
- **Celebrate your successes.** As you achieve milestones in your goals, take the time to celebrate your successes. This will help to keep your employees motivated and engaged.

Maintaining open lines of communication between the employer and employees is important. This means that there should be a way for employees to communicate their concerns and ideas to management, and that management should be willing to listen to and address those concerns.

Policies should not be discriminatory and should be administered uniformly and fairly to all employees regardless of their position or status in the organization.

In going through renewal, organizations need to provide outlets for employees to express themselves. It is important to give employees a chance to share their thoughts and feelings about the changes that are happening, and to make sure that their voices are heard.

Organizations can also schedule periodic debriefing sessions to discuss progress and share thoughts. This is a good way to keep employees informed about what is happening, and to get their feedback on the changes that are being made.

Training should be an ongoing process for organizations for both newly hired workers and long serving staff. Organizations must try to establish their own immersion and certification programs, along with training materials and manuals for various job procedures. It is crucial for an organization to examine whether it needs committed staff members to specific projects and emerging tasks while considering new initiatives and innovations. The ability of an organization's existing workforce to take on new tasks should always be evaluated. A lack of this evaluation leads to snowballing tasks to the cost of the health and emotional well-being of their most performing staff, which is a common mistake organization make. They may continue to load staff that have proven competencies in a number of distinctive areas, while at the same time failing to shed off tasks from those staff.

Employee Responsibility

The process of transformation does not start with other people. It starts with each individual employee. This means that each employee must be willing to change and grow. It also means that each employee must take responsibility for their own actions and the actions of their team.

The processes of change or transformation is given new vitality when self-engagement is present. This means that people are more likely to be motivated and engaged in change when they feel like they have a say in the process. It also means that people are more likely to be successful in change when they are committed to the process.

Both employers and employees need to be willing to listen to each other and consider each other's ideas. It also means that both parties need to be willing to compromise. Both employers and employees must devote time to implementing their proposals. It also means that both parties must be patient and persistent, because change takes time. Leaders must make it possible for people to follow them. They need to carve strong relationships with coworkers and refrain from abusing their positions and authority.

Admitachew said,

> As the organization's leader, I should assume the leadership role. I should also include the governors, who are non-executive and responsible for formulating policies, rules, and providing strategic direction. The second is that I should take the lead by involving and enlisting others. I should therefore take the helm. (Admitachew, personal communication, October 24, 2022)

Informed by the interviewees responses, the following figure depicts roles employees may play to promote emotional wellbeing, and goodwill dissent.

Employees Role in Promoting Constructive Workplace
Dissent, Psychological Safety, and Joy at Work

Respondents Suggestions of What Their Role May Be in Promoting Constructive Workplace Dissent, Psychological Safety and Joy at Work

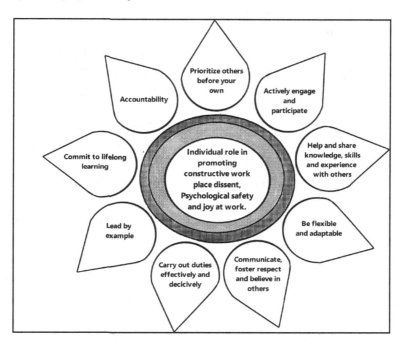

It is imperative to put the needs of other people and of the organization ahead of one's own desires. Accountability is expected of both employees and employers. The implementation of ideas requires active involvement from both employers and employees. It is expected of staff members to actively participate in meetings by offering input, speaking up for their ideas, and embracing constructive criticism. Employees must also put forth effort in carrying out duties effectively and decisively, helping others, imparting knowledge, training and teaching others. Employers and employees must communicate with coworkers, foster respect for and belief in one another, and encourage constructive criticism of other employees' ideas. Employees must be willing to share their skills, knowledge and experience.

Others Responsibility

Interviewees suggested that people should be allowed to participate and contribute to the process of developing a suitable work culture. Herbert said,

I will be very cautious in saying people will be involved in 1, 2, 3, 4 ways but just rather point the direction and where we want to go, and what we want our organization to look like, a place where we all flourish. Then just ask the others to say how can we do that. Experience is that people have experienced discomfort and people express disagreements in the corridors, and for some joy at work is fictitious. They already know what is not working. The best way to have them participate is rather to open it up and say let us create it, so what will it look like, and leave it open like that, and allow every idea just to come on board. There you also get to see concerns. That is how I will say others may contribute. There again it rests on leadership. (K. Herbert, personal communication, October 24, 2022)

Management needs to include others in decision-making. Certainly, others must be enlisted in accordance with their areas of interest, aptitude, and experience. An organization is not the possession of a single person; rather, its leaders, employees and the people it serves share it.

In response to the question "What do you see as the role of others in promoting goodwill dissent, emotional wellbeing and joy at work?" interviewees suggested the following.

Respondents Suggestions on the Role of Others in Promoting Goodwill Dissent, Emotional Wellbeing and Joy at Work

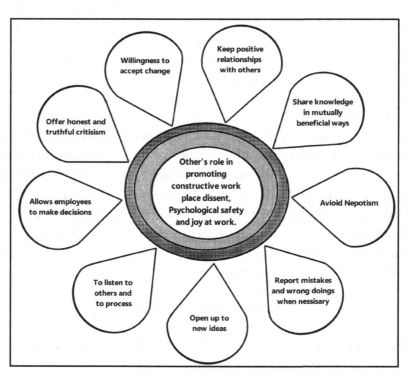

Co-workers and employers need to keep positive connections and relationships. They must be prepared to share knowledge in mutually beneficial ways and must be willing to report mistakes and wrongdoings. Co-workers need to support the system and teamwork through actively participating in meetings, opening up to new ideas, putting aside differences, influencing others, and providing a shoulder to lean on when others seek help and when they share their experiences. Others must also avoid nepotism, be accountable, and be willing to accept change. They also need to listen to others and processes, getting involved and staying involved, and follow up on suggestions made to them by team members. Employees must be allowed to make decisions. Others must also offer honest and truthful criticism.

Below are some additional tips for co-workers and employers who want to keep positive connections and relationships:

- **Be respectful:** Treat each other with respect, even when you disagree.
- **Be open to communication:** Be willing to listen to each other, share ideas, and give feedback.
- **Be honest and reliable:** Keep promises, follow through on commitments, and be transparent about your actions.
- **Be supportive:** Offer help and assistance when needed, celebrate successes, and be there for each other during difficult times.
- **Be forgiving:** Everyone makes mistakes. Be willing to forgive each other and move on.
- **Be positive:** Focus on the positive aspects of your relationship and work together to overcome challenges.
- **Be grateful:** Appreciate each other and the work that you do together.

A KEY TAKEAWAY

DEPICTION OF ABUNDANCE AND DEFICIT MINDSETS FOCUS OF APPRECIATIVE INQUIRY (AI)

Excellence in the workplace should not be an afterthought but rather the default mindset. Instead of starting from a place of deficit and working backward, both employer and employees should always start with what they have to be grateful for (abundance mindset). The value and difficulty of cultivating a mindset of abundance as a matter of course is the issue leaders must address in their organizations.

> Finally, believers, whatever is true, whatever is honorable *and* worthy of respect, whatever is right *and* confirmed by God's word, whatever is pure *and* wholesome, whatever is lovely *and* brings peace, whatever is admirable *and* of good repute; if there is **any excellence,** if there is anything worthy of praise, think *continually* on these things [center your mind on them, and implant them in your heart]. The things which you have learned and received and heard and seen in me, practice these things [in daily life], and the God [who is the source] of peace *and* well-being will be with you. (Philippians 4:8-9)

Chapter 10

EMOTIONAL WELLBEING, GOODWILL DISSENT, HUMAN FLOURISHING (EGH)

DEPICTION OF THE EGH PYRAMID

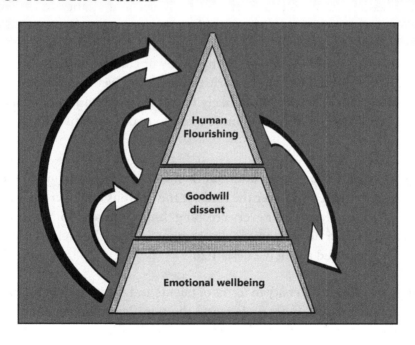

The epiphany moment during my research (which is the basis of this book) was when I realized that emotional wellbeing (psychological safety) could be the foundation on which goodwill dissent (constructive workplace dissent) may stand, and that when goodwill dissent becomes entrenched in an organization's culture, it has the potential to actualize human flourishing (joy at work). This is fascinating. When employees feel safe sharing their ideas and concerns, they are more likely to do so.

Goodwill dissent can have a positive impact on human flourishing (joy at work). When employees feel like they can contribute to their organization and make a difference, they are more likely to be engaged and satisfied with their work. This can lead to a more fulfilling and meaningful life.

However, goodwill dissent is not always easy. It can be difficult to challenge the status quo, and it can be even more difficult to do so in a constructive way. However, with a willing heart it is doable, especially with conviction and practice.

Emotional wellbeing, or psychological safety, is a critical factor that can contribute to a positive and productive workplace culture. When employees feel safe to express their opinions and views without judgment or fear of retribution, they are more likely to engage in constructive workplace dissent.

Emotional wellbeing can directly contribute to flourishing workplaces. By providing employees with the resources and support they need to manage stress, anxiety and other emotional challenges, organizations can create a culture of resilience and vitality. When employees feel valued, supported, and cared for, they are more likely to experience job satisfaction, loyalty, and commitment to the organization.

Emotional wellbeing is not just about feeling happy or content. It is also about feeling safe, secure, and valued. Organizations that prioritize emotional wellbeing are more likely to be successful in the long run. They are more likely to attract and retain top talent, and they are more likely to be profitable. They are also more likely to make a positive impact on the world.

Then God said,

> Let us make man in our image, after our likeness. And let them have dominion over the fish of the sea and over the birds of the heavens and over the livestock and over all the earth and over every creeping thing that creeps on the earth. So, God created man in his own image, In the image of God he created him; male and female he created them. (Genesis 1:26-27)

Recognizing and valuing diversity in terms of talents and equity is crucial in any workplace. Both employers and employees must understand the significance of each individual's unique abilities and perspective, regardless of their position or standing within the hierarchy of any organization. It is imperative to acknowledge and appreciate the image of God in the another. By embracing and celebrating diverse talents, workplaces can foster an environment that is conducive to success.

Some of the key recommendations to promote EGH are as follows:

Employee participation: When employers are concerned about goodwill dissent, emotional wellbeing, and joy at work, it is essential that these qualities are created via the efforts of both employers and employees. Encourage participation from employees so that a culture can be developed collectively with the employer.

Below are some benefits of employee participation:

- *Increased productivity:* When employees feel they are part of the decision-making process, they are more likely to be engaged and committed to their work.
- *Improved innovation:* When employees are given the opportunity to share their ideas, they may come up with new and innovative solutions to challenges.
- *Increased employee satisfaction:* When employees feel they are part of the team and that their contributions are valued, they are more likely to be satisfied with their jobs.
- *Reduced turnover:* When employees are happy with their jobs, they are less likely to leave the organization.
- *Improved morale:* When employees feel like they are part of the team and that their contributions are valued, they are more likely to have high morale.
- *Increased customer satisfaction:* When employees are happy with their jobs, they are more likely to provide a good service to stakeholders.

Allow speaking up:

When an organization functions in an atmosphere where employees are afraid to speak up, where staff are constantly holding back, even for the best ideas they may have, then organizations will be shooting themselves in the foot. It is imperative that organizations do away with punishments that may discourage employees from voicing their disagreements.

There are a number of things that organizations can do to create a more open and inclusive work environment. One is to encourage employees to speak up at meetings and in other forums. Another is to create a culture of feedback, where employees feel comfortable giving and receiving feedback on their work. Organizations can also provide training on how to give and receive feedback effectively.

It is important for organizations to create a culture of trust. Employees need to feel like they can trust their managers and colleagues to listen to them and take their concerns seriously. If employees feel that their concerns are not being heard, they are less likely to speak up.

Encourage healthy competition:

Healthy competition among employees fosters an environment where ideas can emerge from any level of the organization, not just the top brass. A healthy competitive environment not only supports and encourages collaboration, but an understanding that employees' skill sets are complementary rather than adversarial. If employees feel they are being pitted against each other, it can create a hostile work environment and lead to decreased productivity.

Cast the goal:

Developing a shared understanding of the end goal and then letting people choose their own path to attain that goal is a great way to foster innovation and creativity. This allows employees to have a contribution in how their work is done, and not to be constrained by traditional methods or procedures.

Of course, there are some risks associated with this approach. If employees are not given enough guidance, they may end up going in the wrong direction or wasting time on unproductive activities. It is important to strike a balance between giving employees enough freedom to be creative and providing them with enough structure to stay on track.

Releasing control:

By letting go, employers and employees liberate themselves but also those around them. Fears need to be confronted and analyzed by both employers and workers. With less doubt, as worries and fears go away, a brand-new setting emerges. Releasing control is a difficult but a necessary step in personal and professional growth. When leaders let go of their need to control everything, they open themselves up to new possibilities and experiences. When leaders release control, they trust that things will work out. They are also trusting themselves and their ability to adapt to change. This can be a scary thing, but it is also an incredibly liberating thing. Releasing control is a journey, not a destination. It is a process of learning to trust oneself and let go of the need to control everything. It is not always easy, but it is always worth it.

If you are struggling to release control, below are a few ideas:

- **Start small.** Do not try to change everything all at once. Start by letting go of small things, and then gradually work your way up to bigger things.
- **Be patient.** It takes time to learn to let go of control. Do not get discouraged if you do not see results immediately.
- **Be kind to yourself.** It is okay to make mistakes. Just learn from them and keep moving forward.
- **Trust yourself.** You know what is best for you. Trust your gut and follow your intuition.

Policies: When organizations believe in goodwill dissent, joy at work and psychological safety, policy must become a mechanism to remove obstacles that prevent people from expressing themselves. Policies are also a way of institutional memory and organizational aspirations. Goodwill dissent, psychological safety, and joy at work concepts must be ingrained in policy to infuse them into the lifeblood of organizations. Policies should be designed to remove obstacles that prevent people from expressing themselves, and to create a culture where people feel safe to take risks and try new things.

Hierarchy:

Unnecessary organizational layers may keep employees further away from the leaders. Allowing access to and for all levels can be accomplished by making structures somewhat flatter.

In recent years, there has been a growing trend towards flatter organizational structures. This means that there are fewer levels in the hierarchy, and employees have more direct access to decision-makers.

Value system:

The importance of defining organizational values cannot be overstated. Employers should articulate, instruct, and serve as role models for the values they stand for, by exemplifying them. Since many organizations today use the same wording on values, it is especially crucial to define what they mean in a specific organization.

Organizational values are the core principles and beliefs that guide the actions and decision-making processes within an organization. They reflect the organization's culture and vision, shaping the behavior and attitudes of its employees.

One of the primary reasons for establishing clear organizational values is to create a shared understanding of the organization's identity and purpose. When employees are aware of the values that their organization stands for, they can better align their actions and decisions with these principles. This shared understanding fosters a sense of unity and commitment, which can lead to increased employee engagement, satisfaction, and loyalty. Moreover, when organizational values are clearly defined and communicated, it helps create a strong employer brand, attracting potential employees who share the same beliefs and ideals. Given the importance of organizational values, it is essential for employers to take specific steps to define, communicate, and embody them.

The following ideas can be helpful in ensuring that organizational values are effectively implemented and ingrained in an organization's culture:

1. **Identify core values:** The organization must begin by identifying the core values, without which, their organization is not. These values must be aligned with the organization's mission, vision, and strategic objectives.
2. **Define the values:** Once the core values have been identified, it is crucial to define what they mean within the organization's context. This involves providing clear and specific explanations that can guide employees in their understanding and interpretation of these values. The employer should also consider sharing examples and stories that demonstrate how these values can be applied in real-life situations.
3. **Communicate and promote the values:** Employers should communicate and promote the organizational values consistently and effectively. This can be achieved through various channels, such as during employee training programs, internal communications,

organizational events, social media platforms among others. By consistently reinforcing these values, employers can ensure that they become an integral part of the organization's culture.

4. **Lead by example:** It is crucial for employers and leaders within the organization to exemplify the values. By embodying organizational values in their actions and decisions, leaders can serve as role models and inspire employees to adopt the same principles. This can lead to a more cohesive, committed, and value-driven workforce.

Reference List

Adler-Milstein, J., Singer, S.J., & Toeffel, M.W. (2010). Speaking up constructively: Managerial practices that elicit solutions from front-line employees. *Harvard Business School Working Paper* 11-005 https://www.researchgate.net/profile/Sara-Singer/publication/46475701_Speaking_up_constructively_Managerial_practices_that_elicit_solutions_from_front-line_employees/links/09e4150c76a1c82eea000000/Speaking-up-constructively-Managerial-practices-that-elicit-solutions-from-front-line-employees.pdf?_sg%5B0%5D=started_experiment_milestone&origin=journalDetail

Alemu, B. (2018). *The Effect of Internal Communication on Employees Engagement: The Case of Commercial Bank of Ethiopia (CBE).* [Master thesis].
Addis Ababa University School of Commerce. http://etd.aau.edu.et/handle/123456789/16557\

Ashford, S. J., Sutcliffe, K. M., & Christianson, M. K. (2009). Speaking up and speaking out: The leadership dynamics of voice in organizations. In J. Greenberg, & M.S. Edwards (Eds.), *Voice and silence in organizations*, (pp.175-202). https://books.google.com.et/books?hl=en&lr=&id=g1Jqudz41ZIC&oi=fnd&pg=PA175&dq=Ashford+et+al.,+2009+silence&ots=f7TCdATY5P&sig=furX0xSVnfzx-5MDDYmHRwOWWaQ&redir_esc=y#v=onepage&q=Ashford%20et%20al.%2C%202009%20silence&f=false

Bakke, D. (2005). *Joy at work.* PVG.

Bakke, D. (2013). *The decision-maker: Unlock the potential of everyone in your organization, one decision at a time.* Pear Press.

Bayih, B.E. (2018). Potentials and challenges of religious tourism development in Lalibela, Ethiopia. *African Journal of Hospitality, Tourism and Leisure, 7*(4),1-17. https://www.researchgate.net/publication/338866942_Potentials_and_Challenges_of_Religious_Tourism_Development_in_Lalibela_Ethiopia

Bakke Graduate University. (2016). *Transformational leadership perspectives taught at BGU.* Retrieved April 18, 2022, from https://bgu.edu/programs/transformational-leadership-perspectives

Bauer, T. (2015). *What if being happy at work is all just a huge scam?* The Context of things. Retrieved June 12, 2022 from https://thecontextofthings.com/2015/07/22/happy-at-work-is-a-scam/

Berhanu, G. (2006). Intercultural mediation", the institution of learning and the process of educational 'integration' and assimilation: The case of Ethiopian Jews in Israel. *Educational Research and Reviews, 1*(3), 62-79. https://academicjournals.org/article/article1379590000_Berhanu.pdf

Beyene, K.T., Shi, C.S., & Wu, W.W. (2016). Linking culture, organizational learning orientation and product innovation performance: The case of Ethiopian manufacturing firms. *South African Journal of Industrial Engineering, 27*(1), 88-101. http://dx.doi.org/10.7166/27-1-1334

Bolman, L. G., & Deal, T. E. (2017). *Reframing organizations: Artistry, choice, and leadership.* (6th ed.). Jossey-Bass.

Brainy Quote. (n.d). *It always seems impossible until it's done.* Retrieved November 26, 2022, from https://www.brainyquote.com/quotes/nelson_mandela_378967

Brown, L. (n.d.). *Quotes, Quotable quotes.* Retrieved December 02, 2022, from https://www.goodreads.com/quotes/884712-the-graveyard-is-the-richest-place-on-earth-because-it

Burris, E.R. (2012). The risks and rewards of speaking up: Managerial responses to employee voice. *Academy of Management Journal, 55*(4), 851–875. http://dx.doi.org/10.5465/amj.2010.0562

Bushe, G.R. (2007). *Appreciative inquiry is not about the positive.* Retrieved May 29, 2022, from https://zeno-organisatieontwikkeling.nl/zeno/wp-content/uploads/2020/10/Bushe-GR-2007-AI-is-not-about-the-Positive.pdf

Cairn Centre for University Studies. (2014, March 03). *A conversation with Ray Bakke* [Video]. YouTube. https://www.youtube.com/watch?v=bnGarkAbu10

Campeau, M. (2016). Positive dissent. *HR Professional Now.* Retrieved May 29, 2022, from http://hrprofessionalnow.ca/culture/342-positive-dissent

Centre for Creative Leadership. (n.d.). *What is psychological safety at work?* Retrieved April 28, 2022, from https://www.ccl.org/articles/leading-effectively-articles/what-is-psychological-safety-at-work/

Chakamba, R. (2021). *Exclusive: Audit finds nepotism, corruption, and worse at the African Union Commission.* Retrieved April 28, 2022, from https://www.devex.com/news/exclusive-audit-finds-nepotism-corruption-and-worse-at-the-african-union-commission-99181

Clark, T.R. (2021). *What psychological safety is not.* Retrieved May 10, 2022, from https://www.forbes.com/sites/timothyclark/2021/06/21/what-psychological-safety-is-not/?sh=6d7b3fc56452

CMC Canada. (2019). *The value of appreciative inquiry: Focus on strengths not just weaknesses.* Retrieved September 20, 2022 from https://www.cmc-canada.ca/blog/Our%20Blog/the-value-of-appreciative-inquiry

Colon, G. (2012). Incarnational community-based ministry: A leadership model for community transformation. *Journal of Applied Leadership, 6*(2), 10 – 17. Retrieved May 14, 2022 from https://digitalcommons.andrews.edu/cgi/viewcontent.cgi?article=1104&context=jacl

Cooperrider, D.L., & Whitney, D. (2005*). Appreciative inquiry: A positive revolution in change.* Berrett-Koehler Publishers.

Craig, T.B. (2014). *Leveraging the power of loyal dissent in the U.S. Army,* (November – December), 97 -101. Retrieved April 21, 2022, from Military Review - Google Books.

Creswell, J. W., & Creswell, J. D. (2017). *Research design: Qualitative, quantitative, and mixed methods approaches.* (5th ed.). SAGE Publications.

Cultural Atlas. (n.d.). The cultural atlas. Retrieved May 14, 2022, from https://culturalatlas.sbs.com.au/

Dağlı, A. (2017). Investigating the relationship between organizational dissent and life satisfaction. *Universal Journal of Educational Research, 5*(4), 600-607. Retrieved April 25, 2022, from https://files.eric.ed.gov/fulltext/EJ1137680.pdf

Delizonna, L. (2017). High performing teams need psychological safety, here's how to create it. *Harvard Business Review.* Retrieved June 10, 2022, from https://hbr.org/2017/08/high-performing-teams-need-psychological-safety-heres-how-to-create-it.

Deloitte Center for the Edge. (2016). *Shift index; The paradox of flows: Can hope flow from fear?* Retrieved May 09, 2022, from https://www2.deloitte.com/content/dam/insights/us/articles/3407_2016-Shift-Index/DUP_2016-Shift-Index.pdf

Detert, J. R., & Treviño, L. K. (2010). Speaking up to higher-ups: How supervisors and skip-level leaders influence employee voice. *Organization Science, 21*(1), 249–270. https://www.researchgate.net/profile/James-Detert/publication/220521101_Speaking_Up_to_Higher-Ups_How_Supervisors_and_Skip-Level_Leaders_Influence_Employee_Voice/links/5474a53b0cf29afed60f8cc9/Speaking-Up-to-Higher-Ups-How-Supervisors-and-Skip-Level-Leaders-Influence-Employee-Voice.pdf

Drucker, P.F., Collins, J., Kotler, P., Kouzes, J., Rodin, J., Rangan, V.K., Hesselbein, F. (2008). *The five most important questions you will ever ask about your organization.* Leader to Leader Institute.

Edmondson, A. (2020, August 5). *The importance of psychological safety* [Video]. https://www.youtube.com/watch?app=desktop&v=eP6guvRt0U0

Franklin, K.J. (2020). Searching for shalom: Transformation in the mission of God and the Bible translation movement, *HTS Teologiese Studies/ Theological Studies,* 76(4), 4-10. https://www.researchgate.net/publication/341506720_Searching_for_shalom_Transformation_in_the_mission_of_God_and_the_Bible_translation_movement

Fisher, C.D. (2010). Happiness at work. *International Journal of Management Reviews, 12*(4), 384 – 412. Retrieved June 8, 2022, from https://www.researchgate.net/publication/227533694_Happiness_at_Work

Great Place to Work. (n.d.). *The definition of a great place to work.* Retrieved August 5, 2022, from https://www.greatplacetowork.com/trust-model

Guven, C. (2011). Are happier people better citizens?, *Kyklos, 64*(2), 178-192. https://www.researchgate.net/publication/272088573_Are_Happier_People_Better_Citizens

Hirschi, A., Keller, A.C., & Spurk, D. (2017). Living one's calling: Job resources as a link between having and living a calling. *Journal of Vocational Behavior, 106,* 1-10. https://www.researchgate.net/publication/321527329_Living_One's_Calling_Job_Resources_as_a_Link_Between_Having_and_Living_a_Calling

Hundera, A. (2019). Managing workplace conflicts in business environment: The role of Alternative Dispute Resolution (ADR) Ethiopian in focus. *Research Journal of Finance and Accounting, 10* (1), 1-6. https://issuu.com/alexanderdecker/docs/managing_workplace_conflicts_in_bus

James, R. (2012). *Inspiring Change: Creating more space for grace in organizations.* Digni.

Jetu, F.T., Riedl, R., Roithmayr, F. (2011). Cultural patterns influencing project team behavior in Sub-Saharan Africa: A case study in Ethiopia. *Project Management Journal, 42 (5),* 57–77. http://relaunch.rene-riedl.at/wp-content/uploads/2018/02/jetu-et-al-2011.pdf

Kish-Gephart, J.J., Detert, J.R., Trevino, L.K., & Edmondson, A.C. (2009). Silenced by fear: The nature, sources, and consequences of fear at work. *Research in Organizational Behavior, 29,* 163–193. https://www.researchgate.net/publication/238382691_Silenced_by_fear

Maggay, M. P. (2011). *Transforming society: Reflections on the kingdom and politics.* (Repr. ed.). Wipf and Stock Publishers.

Martins, J. (2021). What is constructive criticism? *Asana.* Retrieved May 02, 2022, from https://asana.com/resources/constructive-criticism

Martinuzzi, B. (2019). *The most common seven leadership styles and how to find your own.* Retrieved September 27, 2022, from https://oneteamplaybook.org/wp-content/uploads/2020/10/Leadership-styles-Lydia-Rojas-LearningToLead-Spn.pdf

Merriam, S. B., & Tisdell, E.J. (2016). *Qualitative research: A guide to design and implementation* (4th ed.). Jossey-Bass.

Merriam-Webster. (n.d.). Talent(s). In *Merriam-Webster.com dictionary.* Retrieved May 4, 2022, from https://www.merriam-webster.com/dictionary/TALENTED

Milliken, F.J., Morrison, E.W., & Hewlin, P. F. (2003). *An exploratory study of employee silence: issues that employees don't communicate upward and why?.* Retrieved May 14, 2022, from https://dokumen.tips/documents/an-exploratory-study-of-employee-silence-exploratory-study-of-employee-silence.html?page=1

Morrison, E.W. (2014). Employee Voice and Silence. *Annual Review of Organizational Psychology and Organizational Behaviour, 2014 (1)*, 173-197. Retrieved May 30, 2022 from https://www.annualreviews.org/doi/abs/10.1146/annurev-orgpsych-031413-091328

Naber, A. (n.d.). *One third of your life is spent at work.* Gettysburg College. Retrieved May 14, 2022, from https://www.gettysburg.edu/news/stories?id=79db7b34-630c-4f49-ad32-4ab9ea48e72b#:~:text=The%20average%20person%20will%20spend%2090%2C000%20hours%20at%20work%20over%20a%20lifetime

Perlow, L.A., & Williams, S. (2003). *When silence spells trouble at work.* Harvard Business School. Retrieved May 12, 2022, from https://hbr.org/2003/05/is-silence-killing-your-company

Reju, O. (2022, July, 9). *Servant & calling based leadership* [PowerPoint slides]. Bakke Graduate University.

Rogers P.J., & Fraser, D. (2003) Appreciating appreciative inquiry. *New Directions for Evaluation,* 75 – 83. Retrieved May 16, 2022, from https://fliphtml5.com/ornh/mncd/basic

Ruyter, D., Oades, L., & Waghid, Y. (2021). Meaning of human flourishing and education: research brief by the International Science and Evidence Based Education Assessment, and initiative by UNESCO MGIE. *The Blue Dot, 13,* 54 – 58. Retrieved July 4, 2022, from https://unesdoc.unesco.org/ark:/48223/pf0000375571?posInSet=2&queryId=84896d88-79b6-4a07-92a4-82a6352fa98d

Santy, Katelyn L. (2013). *Where loyalties lie: A study of workplace dissent through the lens of loyalty* (Publication no. 544) [Masters dissertation, University of Northern Iowa]. https://scholarworks.uni.edu/cgi/viewcontent.cgi?article=1603&context=etd

Seligman, M.E.P. (2005). Positive psychology progress: Empirical validation of interventions. *American Psychologist, 60*(5), 410-421. Retrieved May 1, 2022, from https://www.researchgate.net/publication/7701091_Positive_Psychology_Progress_Empirical_Validation_of_Interventions

Sensing, T. (2011). *Qualitative research: A multi-methods approach to projects for Doctor of Ministry theses.* WIPF & Stock.

Shapiro. (n.d.). *Smart leadership means nourishing existing talent.* SNI. Retrieved June 02, 2022, from https://www.shapironegotiations.com/smart-leadership-means-nourishing-existing-talent/

SHRME. (n.d.) *Who we are.* Retrieved December 4, 2022, from https://www.shrme.org/index.php/who-we-are

Sijbom, R., Janssen. O., & Van Yperen, N.W. (2015). Leaders' receptivity to subordinates' creative input: The role of achievement goals and composition of creative input. *European Journal of Work and Organizational Psychology, 24 (3),* 462–478. http://dx.doi.org/10.1080/1359432X.2014.964215

Spicer, A., & Cederstrom, C. (2015). The research we've ignored about happiness at work. *Harvard Business Review.* Retrieved May 17, 2022, from https://hbr.org/2015/07/the-research-weve-ignored-about-happiness-at-work

Thomas, L. (2022). *What is psychological safety?* Friday. Retrieved May 1, 2022, from https://friday.app/p/what-is-psychological-safety

Trompenaars, F., and Hampden-Turner, C. (2012). *Riding the waves of culture: Understanding diversity in global business.* McGraw-Hill Education.

Unler, E., & Sibel C. (2019). Individual and managerial predictors of the different forms of employee voice. *Journal of Management Development, 38* (7), 582-603. Retrieved May 2, 2022, from https://www.researchgate.net/publication/335012081_Individual_and_managerial_predictors_of_the_different_forms_of_employee_voice

About the Author

Gorden Simango (DTL), is an experienced and accomplished human rights, governance, peace, and humanitarian transformational leader with an adherent passion to bring voices from the margins to the centres of power and decision-making, including through enhancing the capacities of local partners in advocacy and policy influencing to promote sustainable development, peace, resilience, and social cohesion. He has worked globally, impacting development policy, international human rights discourse, and humanitarian advocacy and relief. A Zimbabwean, Gorden holds a Bachelor of Arts (double major i. Development Studies ii. Public Administration) from the University of South Africa, a Master of Arts in Leadership and Management from the University of Zimbabwe through the Africa Leadership and Management Academy (ALMA), Post Graduate Certificate, Post Graduate Diploma & a Master of Laws (LLM) Degree from the University of London. He earned his Doctor of Transformational Leadership in Entrepreneurial Organizational Transformation with Honors from Bakke Graduate University in the USA in March 2023. At the time of publishing this book Gorden was serving as Director for the African Union Office & Advocacy at the All Africa Conference of Churches (AACC) based in Addis Ababa, Ethiopia, changed with promoting cooperation with the African Union and its component institutions, the diplomatic community, the United Nations, other international actors and civil society, including advocacy capacity strengthening of AACC members.

Printed in the United States
by Baker & Taylor Publisher Services